Behalf

Behalf

P. N. Furbank

UNIVERSITY OF NEBRASKA PRESS : LINCOLN & LONDON

Chapter 2 was previously published as "On Pluralism" in *Raritan* 17, no.1 (summer 1997): 83–95. The quotation from "The Noodle-Vendor's Flute" on pages 4–5 is reprinted from D. J. Enright, *Collected Poems,* by permission of D. J. Enright; the original publisher, Oxford University Press; and Watson, Little Limited, licensing agents. The quotation from "Everlasting Flowers for a Dead Mother" by D. H. Lawrence on page 37 is from *The Complete Poems of D. H. Lawrence,* by D. H. Lawrence, edited by V. de Sola Pinto and F. W. Roberts. Copyright © 1964, 1971 by Angelo Ravagli and C. M. Weekley, Executors of the Estate of Frieda Lawrence Ravagli. Used by permission of Viking Penguin, a division of Penguin Putnam Inc., Laurence Pollinger Limited, and the Estate of Frieda Lawrence Ravagli.

Library of Congress Cataloging-in-Publication Data
Furbank, Philip Nicholas. Behalf / P.N. Furbank. p. cm. Includes bibliographical references and index. ISBN 0-8032-2009-X (cl. : alk. paper) 1. Political science – Philosophy. 2. Humanism. 3. Pluralism (Social sciences). I. Title. JA71.F87 1999 320'.01'1—dc21 98-51178 CIP

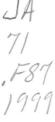

For Graham Martin

Contents

1 A Rule of Behavior   1

2 "Pluralism"   11

3 "We," "Us," and "I"   25

4 Race and Nationalism   41

5 Behalf   57

6 The Politics of Gender   73

7 Humanisms   83

8 Antihumanisms   91

9 Politics, New Style and Old   111

   Notes   117

   Index   121

Behalf

1

A Rule of Behavior

Marcel Proust, in *Le Temps retrouvé*, wrote that "in reality every reader, while he is reading, is the reader of his own self." The writer's work, according to this theory, "is merely a kind of optical instrument which he offers to the reader to enable him to discern what, without this book, he would perhaps never have perceived in himself." It is implicit in Proust's idea that each human being comprises, potentially, the characteristics of the whole human species. Proust's narrator even goes on to speculate, fantastically, whether there may not be just one intelligence in the whole world, with human individuals as its cotenants: "an intelligence onto which everyone, from their particular body, directs their gaze, as in the theatre where, though everyone has a seat, there is only a single stage-scene."

There is something akin to Proust's view in the way that, in the preface to *The Nigger of the Narcissus*, Joseph Conrad connects the artist's act of introspection with human solidarity – "the subtle but invincible conviction of solidarity that knits together the loneliness of innumerable hearts." The implication is that every individual is an all-inclusive monad: that he or she is committed to fellow-feeling, not so much for philanthropic reasons as because potentially he or she incorporates the human race. He is asserting something not too different from what D. H. Lawrence once declared in a letter to Bertrand Russell: "The ultimate passion of every man is to be within himself the whole of mankind."

It will be seen that what is involved here is a form of humanism. "Humanism" and "solidarity" are words liable to get one into trouble, from more than one quarter. Nevertheless, at least one of the rules that humanism prescribes strikes me as being of inestimable value. It is that – in all fields of ethical or political debate – one must not leave oneself out of the equation. There ought to be, one feels, a figure of rhetoric called the "self-excluder." It would help define a very familiar (and very reprehensible) practice, which comes in countless guises. A good example, shall we say, is to employ the term "bourgeois" as if it were purely a category for others – ignoring the all-important fact that the speaker himself or herself must, according to this style of language, belong either to the "bourgeoisie" or the "proletariat" and, presumably, be speaking from that angle. The gibe "listen to who's talking!" can be rather profound.

It is in a way a gibe that might have been made against the Positivists of the Auguste Comte school, who practiced the Religion of Humanity. For to make a religion of Humanity sounds, to the malicious minded, like making a religion of yourself. One remembers, too, the puzzlement of Proust's Swann, when Odette tells him that he has quite misjudged So-and-so in calling him worldly and self-seeking. This person, she says, is really a most pure-souled, poetical, and spiritual man: he has told her so himself.

It is such reasons that make it not seem quite proper for George Steiner to ask us to admire the spectacle of poets going silent, as their response to the Holocaust. For one needs to imagine him, or any critic, coming up to a poet face-to-face and telling him or her how much he approves of their silence – even trying to turn the remark into a pretty compliment. It would be grotesque – a case of forgetting who you are and whom you are talking to. The same might be said of Marx (though he deserves to be called a humanist) when in 1843 he saw hope and redemption for future generations in the very extremity of dispossession, the loss of its very humanity, of the existing proletariat. For imagine a flesh-and-blood intellectual actually asking a flesh-and-blood worker to make a more than Christ-like sacrifice on behalf of posterity. It would be a most fantastic scene. There are things, and this seems to be one of them, that no one is in a position to say.

Let me examine a more elaborate example: Wordsworth and his "Old Cumberland Beggar." The poem is a plea against imprisoning a destitute old vagrant in a workhouse, and its arguments are these (was a more selfish set of reasons ever propounded?). The beggar makes us count our own blessings and realize how well off we are. He encourages us to perform our little acts of charity: a neighbor, though poor herself, gives the beggar a handful of meal every Friday and then,

> Returning with exhilarated heart
> Sits by the fire, and builds her hope
>   of heaven.

Thirdly, we are to let him struggle picturesquely with cold winds and winter snows because the hope in his heart is an emotion worthy of reverence. (But presumably the hope in his heart might have something to do with finding shelter?) Fourthly, we ought to allow the old man the chance to enjoy the pleasant sights and sounds of nature – though in fact he is unable to, being too deaf to hear the birdsong and too bent with rheumatics to look up at the sunset.

The objection here is not quite the same as my earlier one, for Wordsworth is clear about whom he is talking to: he is addressing the government, the parish authorities, and his educated readers, those lovers of the picturesque – certainly not the old man himself. Nevertheless, unless Wordsworth really was a hypocrite on a Chadband-like or Pecksniffian scale, something has gone wrong with his logic here. He is trying to say what he is not in a position to say.

But then, with all his virtues, Wordsworth was not a humanist, nor, essentially, much interested in people. To be a humanist, as to be a Wordsworth, calls for imagination, but of a rather special kind. The duty of a humanist is to ask, or his talent is for asking, "Who is saying what to whom?" and "What are the things that can, or cannot, be said, remembering that

speakers are not angels or extraterrestrial visitants but subject
to the same contractual laws of discourse as their listeners?"

One of the writers today most equipped with this kind of
imagination, and continually grappling with this issue, is the
poet D. J. Enright, and it so happens that a poem of his, "The
Noodle-Vendor's Flute," provides a perfect critique of Wordsworth's "Old Cumberland Beggar."

> In a real city, from a real house,
> At midnight by the ticking clocks,
> In winter by the crackling roads:
> Hearing the noodle-vendor's flute,
> Two single fragile falling notes . . .
> But what can this small sing-song say,
> Under the noise of war?
> The flute itself a counterfeit
> (Siberian wind can freeze the lips),
> Merely a rubber bulb and metal horn
> (Hard to ride a cycle, watch for manholes
> And late drunks, and play a flute together)
> Just squeeze between gloved fingers,
> And the note of mild hope sounds:
> Release, the indrawn sigh of mild despair . . .
> A poignant signal, like the cooee
> Of some diffident souls locked out,
> Less than appropriate to cooling macaroni.
> Two wooden boxes slung across the wheel,
> A rider in his middle age, trundling
> This gross contraption on a dismal road,
> Red eyes and nose and breathless rubber horn.
> Yet still the pathos of that double tune
> Defies its provenance, and can warm
> The bitter night.
> Sleepless, we turn and sleep.
> Or sickness dwindles to some local limb.
> Bought love for one long moment gives itself.

Or there a witch assures a frightened child
She bears no personal grudge.
And I, like other listeners,
See my stupid sadness as a common thing.
And being common,
Therefore something rare indeed.
The puffing vendor, surer than a trumpet,
Tells us we are not alone.
Each night that same frail midnight tune
Squeezed from a bogus flute,
Under the noise of war, after war's noise,
It mourns the fallen, every night,
It celebrates survival —
In real cities, real houses, real time.

Between the situation of Wordsworth's beggar and Enright's noodle vendor, the one struggling "with frosty air and winter snows" and having the "chartered wind" beat his grey locks against his withered face, and the other trundling "cooling macaroni" by night on a potholed ride in a Siberian wind, there is not much to choose; but, on the other hand, the profit we are asked to derive from them is of a very different order. In Enright's vision, the point is, there is no calculation, no profit-and-loss account: the gain is entirely gratuitous, an unexpected blessing or "plus" for which the noodle vendor has neither to be sacrificed nor thanked. The noodle vendor himself is to be treated neither in the romantic nature-poet manner – that is to say, as if he were just a part of the landscape, a rock, or a picturesque wind-bent tree; nor in the utilitarian-moralist manner, in terms of social benefit – in other words, of what one can get out of him. His existence as a particular fellow human being is acknowledged fully, and in a casual and rueful way we are tempted to try it on as a symbol for our own existence; but on the other hand, it is not in the least invaded. It is just that, by an accident (the tune of his absurd little rubber horn) his existence has this power of invading, slipping through bedroom windows, and overcoming even the noise of war. The things that Enright says in this poem, and elsewhere, are the ones that he *is* – and we in his shoes *are* – in a position to say.

It is clear that this question, or this mode of imagination, had large significance for Wittgenstein. Here is what he says about predestination, that is to say, election to salvation or damnation: "*Predestination:* It is only permissible to write like this out of the most dreadful suffering – and then it means something quite different. But for this reason it is not possible for someone to assert it as a truth, unless he himself says it in torment. – It simply isn't a theory. – Or, to put it another way: If this is truth, it is not the truth that seems at first sight to be expressed by these words. It's less a theory than a sigh, or a cry."[1] Wittgenstein is adopting what I have been describing as a "humanist" line of questioning; that is, asking who has the right to say such-and-such a thing, and from what position? It brings home to us the greatness of Bunyan's *Pilgrim's Progress*, in which seeking one's personal salvation is presented altogether ruefully, as a most appalling and agonizing business for any feeling man. It is demanded of the Pilgrim that he shall obey the most shocking and outrageous of all Christ's demands – shall hate wife, parents, children, neighbors, and brethren – in order to follow Christ and pursue his own private salvation. The extraordinary feat of Bunyan's book is to show that, against all expectation, such a belief can bear fruit in attractive human virtues, such as courage, loyalty, shrewdness, and compassion – not to mention some genial human errors. There is a kind of clue to this in Wittgenstein's "and then it means something quite different."

Another, and related, remark of Wittgenstein's also lodges in one's mind, as a truth it will take a long time to get to the bottom of. "Only a very unhappy man," he says, "has the right to pity someone else." One is haunted by this saying when reading about Victorian charity organization, as in Gertrude Himmelfarb's *The Idea of Poverty* and *Poverty and Compassion.*

It is a reminder, for one thing, that pity (if not compassion, which is not quite the same) is a most perilous and outrageous emotion, hardly safe to let loose upon the world. None of us ever wants to be pitied – even if, to score a point, we may complain that our oppressors are "pitiless." Nor, for that matter, do we easily admit someone's right (unless perhaps it be Christ's) to bless us for being poor. It is even hardly decent for a real-life individual, confronting another real-life individual, to think of him or her as "one of the poor," any more than to think of him or her as "one of the masses"; and Wittgenstein, whose phrase is "pity someone else" in the singular, might not have conceded the right to pity "others," in the plural, at all.

It is significant that Tolstoy, one of Wittgenstein's heroes, made an unforgettable examination of pity in action. It was just about the time of the great late-Victorian charity-organization movement in England – the epoch of Charles Booth and William Booth, of that century's "Great Depression" and *The Bitter Cry of Outcast London* – that Tolstoy set forth to encounter the outcast poor of Moscow. "I had spent my life in the country," he writes in *What Then Must We Do?* (1886), "and when in 1881 I came to live in Moscow, the sight of town poverty surprised me." He feels he must investigate it, and, on a freezing December night in 1881, he mingles with the wretched queue outside the Lyapin Free Night-lodging House. Overwhelmed by the spectacle, he begins to distribute the change in his pocket, causing a disagreeable scuffle on the pavement, then he follows the crowd into the lodging house, where he gets rid of the rest of his cash and, feeling as if he had committed a crime, he hurries home to "a five-course dinner served by two lackeys in dress clothes with white ties and white gloves."

Back home, friends tell him it is only his provincialism that makes him see anything extraordinary in it: things are even worse in London. But, he cries, tearfully and angrily, "one cannot live so; one cannot; one cannot!" Alarmed by the noise, his wife comes in: why, they ask, can he never discuss things without getting in a frenzy? The existence of "such unfortunate people," they say, not unreasonably, does not justify his spoiling the lives of the people near to him. He has to agree, and is silenced. The feeling of guilt remains, however; and when he talks more calmly about it to his friends, they tell him his feelings do him great credit. The fact of the matter, they say – and he is inclined to believe them – is that the sight has affected him so strongly because he is a particularly kind and good man.

He returns to the Lyapin lodging house, and to Rzhanov House, the very lower depths of the city; indeed becomes an habitué of these places, but his experience there is discouraging. With the inmates who seem most to deserve help, he finds himself unable to make any real human contact, and anyway their friends seem to be looking after them already; and as for those who allow him to help them – dropouts from "good" families, out-of-place officials, befuddled former officers, people waiting on the result of a certain lawsuit for all things to come right again – they are never an atom better for his assistance. Something is wrong, deeply so, he comes to sense; and indeed he has already half glimpsed what it is. This "particularly good and kind man" Leo Tolstoy, with such precious material, spiritual, and cultural gifts to offer, compares on the whole very badly with the poor. The poor are either too much like him – that is, too weak and drugged with illusions to benefit from charity – or they are better and morally stronger than him and in no need of it.

Nevertheless, he devises a practical philanthropic plan – a fairly cracked-brain one, the reader cannot but observe. Taking advantage of the current census, he will recruit his aristocratic acquaintances to come round with him and with the census takers, thereby gaining a thorough grasp of life in the Moscow slums; and eventually they shall each adopt a certain number of the Moscow poor, thus solving the problem of urban poverty. His friends, when they understand the scheme, are embarrassed, ashamed that he should talk nonsense, "but a kind of nonsense which it was impossible plainly to call non-sense." All the same, they agree to join with him in a visit to Rzhanov House. Tolstoy beautifully catches the absurdity of the scene: "My society acquaintances had dressed specially in shooting jackets and high travelling boots, a costume in which they went on hunting expeditions, and which in their opinion was adapted for a visit to the night-lodging-houses. They took with them peculiar notebooks and extraordinary pencils. They were in that special state of excitement people are in when preparing for a hunt, a duel, or to start for the war." [2]

What Then Must We Do? is a great work, and there is a passage in it that vividly dramatizes the troubled relation of philanthropy to pity. Tolstoy is visiting the prostitutes' quarter in Rzhanov House and, resenting the contemptuous tone of the lodging-house keeper, he replies to him angrily, and with words of pity for the women. Instantly a woman's head, and then another, appears above the cubicle's partition, and he finds the whole room eagerly listening.

An awkward silence ensued. The student who had been smiling became serious; the landlord lowered his eyes abashed; and the women, not drawing a breath, looked at me and waited. I was more abashed than any of them. I had not at all expected that a word casually dropped would produce such an effect. It was as when Ezekiel's field of death strewn with bones quivered at the touch of the spirit and the dead bones moved. I had spoken a chance word of love and pity, and it had acted on all as though they had only been waiting for that word to cease to be corpses and to become alive. [3]

They wait for him to say more, to "speak the words and do the deeds that would cause the bones to come together and be covered with flesh and come to life again," but nothing comes; he cannot go on. In the depths of his soul he feels that he is a fraud – "that I was myself like them and had nothing more to say." Tolstoy here comes close to Wittgenstein's saying, that only a very unhappy man (something that Tolstoy evidently was not) has the right to pity someone else.

9

2

"Pluralism"

W hen political philosophers speak about "humanity" it will often seem they are picturing some vaguely imagined collection of human beings, whereas, if the opening remark in this book is correct, they ought to be thinking of the human *species*, that entity of which every individual is an exemplar. They are looking for "humanity" in the wrong place. This mistake seems particularly common with advocates of political "pluralism."

It is not instantly clear what people mean by "pluralism." Isaiah Berlin, who claims Herder to have been in a sense the inventor of pluralism as a doctrine, defines it in this way: "The belief not merely in the multiplicity, but in the incommensurability, of the values of different cultures and societies and, in addition, in the incompatibility of equally valid ideals, together with the implied revolutionary corollary that the classical notions of an ideal man and of an ideal society are intrinsically incoherent and meaningless."[1] Let us begin with a very general question. What are we to think of that phrase, "the incompatibility of equally valid ideals"? Here Berlin is speaking, not so much of different cultures or societies, as of humankind in general; and it is of course true that human ideals may very well be incompatible. Chastity and free love, or honor-seeking and Christian humility, are, as ideals, not compatible with each other. But this is not what he has in mind, for chastity and free love, and honor-seeking and Christian humility, are directly related to each other as opposites. What he is envisaging, rather, is *unrelated* ideals or values; and one asks oneself, in what sense can ideals be unrelated (have no intrinsic relevance to one another) yet at the same time be necessarily incompatible?

At all events, what is being ignored here is an altogether familiar part of our experience – the occasions when ideals or values, *our own* ideals or values, come into conflict. Suppose that somebody regards truthfulness as an ideal, and also loving-kindness. It is not difficult to imagine a situation in which this person finds the claims of truthfulness (or "brutal candor") at war with those of personal kindness. It is the sort of painful dilemma we are finding ourselves in all the time. I have selected a conflict from everyday life, though of course there are rarer and more tragic ones, like those that faced Huckleberry Finn and Antigone.

Faced with such a problem, what does one do? Knowing that one must make a choice, one refers the choice to instinct – or rather, it would be better to say, to spontaneous feeling. That is to say, we present issues, and all the likely consequences of choosing one way or the other, to our imagination, with all the honesty that we possibly can (this is where the discipline of ethics comes in); and having done this, we wait to see what our heart tells us to do. There is nothing in the least irrational in this process (i.e., in asking oneself "What do I really feel?" "Which set of values means most to me here?" and acting in accordance with the answer). Nor is there any dereliction of moral "principle," for morality comes in in the manner in which one does it. When Huck Finn faced his famous choice, he will have told himself, in thoroughly Kantian fashion, to face it *honestly* – not to let any selfish motive blur the way he presented it to himself.

The thing to get hold of is that conflicts between values, of this kind, are not some sort of freakish anomaly, but are the main stuff of our moral life. It is easy to regard oneself as subscribing, in principle, to this and to that moral value; the hard thinking and serious heart-searching come, exactly, when we find two of these values in conflict. But the fact that these values of ours – "equally valid" values, to use Berlin's words

– sometimes come into conflict does not mean that they are "incompatible." For most of the time they live peacefully side by side with one another, and that is all that can be asked of them; that is all that "compatibility" in this case can be supposed to mean.

This is indeed the conclusion some philosophers come to. Bernard Williams, for instance, broadly takes this standpoint, and so does Thomas Nagel. "It is my view," writes Williams in *Moral Luck*, "that value-conflict is not necessarily pathological at all, but something necessarily involved in human values, and to be taken as central by an adequate understanding of them." [2] Thomas Nagel comes to much the same conclusion in *Mortal Questions*. He holds, very sensibly, that it is an illusion to suppose that all values represent, or can be reduced to, some single ultimate "good." Human beings, as he says, "are complex creatures who can view the world from many perspectives – individual, relational, impersonal, ideal etc. – and each perspective presents a different sort of claims."

All the same – and this is what is puzzling – both Williams and Nagel treat the matter as philosophically disturbing. Williams goes along with Isaiah Berlin's epithet "incommensurable." He holds that, despite various qualifications, there is still "something true and important" in the view that the gains and losses in values entailed in social progress are incommensurable, there being no "common currency" in which they can be computed; that "values, or at least the most basic values, are not only plural but in a real sense incommensurable." But this is odd, for as he himself makes clear, if you spell out the possible senses in which values could be said to be "commensurable," you see at once how fallacious they all are. The truth of the matter is plain, according to Williams:

1. There is no one currency in terms of which each conflict of values can be resolved.

2. It is not true that for each conflict of values, there is some value, independent of any of the conflicting values, which can be appealed to in order to resolve that conflict.

3. It is not true that for each conflict of values, there is some value which can be appealed to (independent or not) in order rationally to resolve that conflict.[3]

From which it might be simpler to conclude that what we have here is no deep philosophical impasse, but rather that the idea of values being "commensurable" or "incommensurable" simply makes no sense.

That there is some kind of muddle here comes out even more vividly in Alasdair MacIntyre's *After Virtue*. MacIntyre, as is well known, puts forward a sort of "World We Have Lost" theory of ethics and politics, turning on the notion that "we" have more or less completely lost any understanding of morality. As, after some gigantic natural catastrophe, people might try to reassemble the disordered fragments of earlier scientific knowledge, uncomprehendingly lumping together phlogiston theory with Einsteinian relativity, so in the twentieth century (according to MacIntyre) we continue to use ethical terms but have lost all grasp of the conceptual scheme that gave them their significance. This scheme he identifies, loosely, with Aristotle's theory of the Virtues – one according to which, says MacIntyre, the concept of "the good life for man" comes before the concept of a virtue. The "good life" is essentially social; it is a "practice with goods internal to itself," involving a notion of the "narrative unity" of a human being's life, and the virtues are those "dispositions" that sustain this practice and the quest for the good. By contrast with this coherently ordered system, he says, in the present age incoherence reigns and "pluralism threatens to submerge us all." Moral debate in the present day is characteristically interminable, and it could scarcely be otherwise, since the arguments used in it suffer from "conceptual incommensurability." Indeed the process of moral debate today is only a masquerade, for underlying it is the view that there are, and can be, no "unassailable criteria" for resolving moral issues. "Emotivism" – that is to say, the doctrine that all evaluative judgments are merely expressions of personal preference – has won the day.

There is a lot to be said about MacIntyre's theory (mostly against it), but one point comes out very neatly from what he says about Aristotle. For, following in the steps of Plato, Aristotle holds that the virtues are unified and inseparable, flourishing side-by-side harmoniously and without conflict in the character of the good man. Now, as MacIntyre himself points out, Aristotle is pitching things rather strong here; for he had only to think of the *Antigone* and the *Philoctetes* of Sophocles to remember that there might be tragic, and in a sense irresolvable, conflicts of values. But of course these tragic conflicts are by no means the only ones needing mention. The virtues on which Aristotle perhaps lays most emphasis of all are Justice and Friendship; and what could be more obvious – more familiar to everyone's experience in whatever society, including the city-states of ancient Greece – than that the claims of justice are sometimes going to clash painfully with the claims of friendship? According to Plutarch's "Life" of Aristides, a difference over this with his rival Themistocles was a dominating factor in the early part of Aristides's career.

Themistocles, joining an association of partisans, fortified himself with considerable strength; insomuch that when someone told him that were he impartial he would make a good magistrate; "I wish," replied he, "I may never sit on that tribunal where my friends shall not plead a greater privilege than strangers." But Aristides walked, so to say, alone on his own path in politics, being unwilling, in the first place, to go along with his associates in ill-doing, or to cause them vexation by not gratifying their wishes; and, secondly, observing that many were encouraged by the support they had in their friends to act injuriously, he was cautious; being of the opinion that the integrity of his words and actions was the only right security for a good citizen.[4]

Reading Plutarch after MacIntyre gives one the feeling of rejoining the real world; and it brings home to us that what we are learning here from Aristotle is not something about ethics and the nature of the good life but about the folly of taking political philosophers literally. (For the fact that Justice and Friendship are sometimes going to come into conflict can hardly have escaped Aristotle.) The function of political philosophy, it serves to remind us, is essentially devious, amounting in many cases – for instance Hobbes, not to mention Leo Strauss and Michael Oakeshott – to what you might call licensed farce. (It would be a naive reader who supposed Hobbes actually believed, or expected anyone else literally to believe, that nothing a sovereign or a master may do can ever be called injustice. This is a notion belonging to the realm of *fantastic* logic, which is where it gets its force.)

Meanwhile, it would seem as if this business of the "conflict of values" might be a false problem – a false problem *philosophically*, though an intensely serious one humanly.

But let us now consider Isaiah Berlin's definition of "pluralism" not in relation to ethics in general, but as a political concept, and in regard to what it says about diversity of cultures. Here, too, one or two things seem not to be good logic. To repeat a point made earlier, what does it mean to speak of the values of different cultures as being "incommensurable"? That is to say, what else could they be? What would it mean, even in theory, for a value to be measured? It must mean, if anything, measuring it against some other value, and this would lead to an infinite regression. (Perhaps, like Nietzsche, one might aspire to "transvalue all values," but that is a different matter.)

The problem comes out more clearly in another passage in the same book of Berlin's, *Vico and Herder:* "What he [Herder] rejects is the single overarching standard of values, in terms of which all cultures, characters, and acts can be evaluated. Each phenomenon to be investigated presents its own measuring rod, its own internal constellation of values in the light of which alone 'the facts' can be truly understood."[5] Berlin is touching here on a favorite theme of his: that Western thought, up to a very late era, has been dominated by the theory (on the part of thinkers of all brands) that there is a single ideal way of life, dedicated to a single supreme value, in which all other values are subsumed. Herder, according to Berlin, was perhaps the first clearly to realize that values might be irredeemably diverse, and that the quest for the one right way of life or ideal society was intrinsically absurd.

There is, one feels, something not quite right in this account. Perry Anderson put it very well in a review of Berlin's *The Crooked Timber of Humanity:* "Can Ancient, or Medieval, or Early Modern society really have been so ideologically monolithic that the possibility of alternative conceptions of a good life was never seriously entertained? At the very outset of his story, Berlin seems to have mislaid Mount Olympus. What was Classical polytheism but the personification of many and contrary values?"[6]

What Berlin is actually saying, one feels, is rather less than it claims. As regards "cultures," all it really amounts to is that each culture or society has to be understood in its own terms and in the light of its own values. That is to say, it is a statement about *understanding,* not about evaluation. No meaning can be attached to the idea of "measuring" (i.e., evaluating) a culture by its own standard of measurement; for a measuring rod, it needs hardly be said, cannot be measured by itself. "Measurement," and hence "incommensurability," do not come into the matter, and the doctrine being attributed to Herder is simple cultural relativism – the view that, though one may try to understand and empathize with a culture not one's own, one must not presume to judge it.

This is, moreover, not an absurd doctrine, and it is even one sometimes proclaimed by anthropologists. But, after reading Lévi-Strauss's great chapter "Un petit verre du rhum" in *Tristes tropiques,* one is likely to regard it as a pious fiction, and an unnecessary one. Lévi-Strauss's answer to the "relativist" is very helpful to us, and it deserves to be set out at some length. He asks: Is not the ethnographer in a hopeless dilemma? He has a society under his very eyes, his own. So why does he devote to *other* societies the patience and devotion he owes to this one? The answer is, that very few ethnographers have a neutral attitude toward their subject. If they are empire builders or missionaries, they are committed to propagating a colonial system. If they are scientists or academics, then the odds are that (for whatever reason) they are misfits in their own society; thus, the value they attach to exotic cultures rests on false foundations, being merely a function of their dislike for their own culture. Subversive among his own people, such ethnographers grow intensely protective and conservative toward an alien culture, simply because it *is* alien. Thus his critics would seem to have an unanswerable case: in finding reasons for preferring an alien culture, is he not in fact appealing to the values of his own culture, and thus indirectly affirming its superiority over all others? It seems as though, to have any claim to be a scientist, he needs to renounce value judgments of any kind and admit that, among the possibilities open to humankind, each society makes its own choice, and these choices are simply not to be compared one with another.

But then, does this mean that the ethnographer must pass no criticism on cruelty, injustice, and deprivation, just because they occur in another society, and even though members of that society protest against them themselves? How can this square with fighting such things in his own country? The problem looks insurmountable; and if it were so, the ethnographer's choice would be clear. "He is an ethnographer, he has chosen to be one; he must accept the mutilation that this entails. He has chosen in favour of 'others' and must suffer the consequences. His role will be merely to understand those others – being precluded from acting in their name, since the very fact that they *are* others prevents him from thinking or desiring in their place and thereby identifying with them. Further, he must renounce action even as regards his own society, for fear of adopting prejudices in regards to values that he may also meet with other societies."[7]

But fortunately, says Lévi-Strauss, the dilemma is not really so complete, and there is a way out, by means of a two-stage process of reasoning. First, it is to be remembered that no society is perfect, even in its own eyes: every society contains by its nature an "impurity" in regard to its own proclaimed norms – an injustice, insensibility, or cruelty according to those norms. Now this is where the ethnographer has something valuable to offer. For when only a few societies are compared with one another they appear extremely different, but on comparing a large number, as an ethnographer does, one finds that no society is without certain advantages for its members, and also that the dose of "impurity" or "iniquity" in societies tends to be fairly constant. (Perhaps it represents a "specific inertia" resisting all efforts at social organization.)

Extended comparison between societies can thus teach moderation and good faith. It is a school for correcting, for instance, a prejudice such as Western societies nurse against cannibalism. To an observer from a different society, the opposite practice, of "vomiting" enemies of society into prisons and the like, might seem equally strange and horrific.

There are, indeed, those who, says Lévi-Strauss, count it the great glory of Western civilization that it, and it alone, has produced ethnographers, but this is a flattering delusion. The truth, more probably, is that it has done so because of the weight of its own sense of guilt (in particular for its treatment of the New World). It produces ethnographers out of a compulsion to reassure itself that other cultures share some of the same ills, and in the hope of finding some explanation for its own. The ethnographer is a symbol of expiation. On the other hand, we should not, out of self-condemnation, allow ourselves to glorify some other culture, whether past or present. That would be the worst dishonesty; for it would be to forget that, if we belonged to that culture, we would find it as intolerable as our own and criticize it for much the same reasons.

Men, says Lévi-Strauss, are born social (the "natural man" being an unnecessary fiction); and all humankind have the same task – to find the formula of a livable society. Other societies are not better than ours, and even if we thought they were, we would have no way of proving it; but getting to know other societies is a way of detaching ourselves mentally from our own, thus putting ourselves in a position to take the "second step." This consists in using other societies to help in identifying the principles of social existence, in order to apply them to reforming our own. For it is only our own society we can change without risking its destruction – the changes that we are introducing coming, in this case, from within it.

As will be seen, far from affirming the incomparability of cultures, à la Herder or Isaiah Berlin, Lévi-Strauss attaches the highest importance to comparing them and to discerning in them various likenesses-across-a-difference. His analysis of the ethnographer's dilemma is, moreover, a magnificent example of what I have called one of the rules of humanism: that one should always be asking oneself what – given one's particular situation vis-à-vis other humans – one has the right, or does not have the right, to say.

Isaiah Berlin represents Herder as holding that human beings flourish only "when the individual is happily integrated into the 'natural community,' which grows spontaneously, like a plant, and is not held together by artificial clamps, or soldered together by sheer force, or regulated by laws and regulations invented, whether benevolently or not, by the despot or his bureaucrats."[8] Each of these "natural societies," in the words of Herder's *Yet Another Philosophy of History,* contains with itself the "ideal of its own perfection, wholly independent of all comparison with those of others."

Here there seems to be involved a further and quite different fallacy: a false idea of the relation of political theory to actual societies. For it is not the case, historically, that societies have organized themselves according to (in Herder's phrase) the "ideal of their own perfection," or as Aristotle would put it, "for some good purpose." "Societies," in the large sense of the word (as opposed, I mean, to things like the Kipling Society, or what Michael Oakeshott liked to call "enterprise associations"), are not created for a *purpose* at all. They come into being through a variety of possible *causes*, short-term and long-term – migration, plague, famine, religious revival, military defeat, or the disintegration of empires. It is not as though someone one day thought up feudalism as the blueprint for an "ideal society." It would only be otherwise, and "societies" would be purpose-built affairs, dedicated to some supreme value, if the founders and first members of new societies had not been living in society up to that moment. But on the contrary, the founder-members of even the most abstractly conceived societies – shall we say the United States, or Soviet Russia – were burdened with a huge baggage of memories, customs, and ancient habits of thought. They arrived on the scene, like Aeneas, with their household gods in their arms. There are, and can be, no truly fresh beginnings in human history. From which it follows that in any society whatever, a great many different "values" or "ideals," expressive of ancient experience, will be active. (Things are different, of course, with a utopia. For a utopia is a blueprint designed for human beings who are assumed to have no past.) That certain of these values may be taken up and glorified by the powers-that-be, and others hounded down with persecuting ferocity, or that some societies are infinitely less tolerant than others, is an all-important matter, but a different one.

Herder's view, moreover, makes us ask ourselves what sense, if any, it makes to speak of a "plural," or "pluralist," society? The phrase would presumably denote a society in which diverse religions, adherences, languages, or sets of customs (perhaps even diverse romantic national aspirations) were able to flourish side by side in amity; and one thing is clear, the last place you will look for such a thing is one of Herder's "natural societies" – the kind that grow "spontaneously like a plant" and are dedicated to "the ideal of their own perfection." They are, by definition, just the sort of society that will bitterly resent such disagreement within its midst. To have a "plural" society, one will require "artificial clamps" and very tough rules, no doubt drawn up by bureaucrats – the very things that Herder is represented as abhorring. Indeed, one might go further. One tends to associate the concept of "pluralism" with liberal thinkers, but it could be argued that it is only likely really to flourish under a despotism. For it may be supposed that, under a regime like that of the Ottoman Turks, so long as a subject kept the peace and paid his taxes, it would be a matter of perfect indifference to his rulers what he believed, or how he worshipped, or what language he spoke. Moreover, the subject would pay his rulers the same compliment. Ernest Gellner has a nice fantasy of a "typical burgher" in an agrarian society, hearing that the local pasha had been overthrown and wondering anxiously whether his successor will be more, or less, grasping and corrupt, more, or less, just and merciful. "If, at that point, his wife dared ask the burgher what language the new Pasha spoke in the intimacy of his home life – was it Arabic, Turkish, Persian, French or English? – the hapless burgher would give her a sharp look, and wonder how he would cope with all his difficulties when, at the same time, his wife had gone quite mad." A "culturally plural" society presents little difficulty, assuming that its members do not expect to play any part in politics; and even in the epoch of industrialization and nationalism, the point to some degree still holds. Some would say that the Austro-Hungarian Empire found a very successful way of handling cultural diversities. The anthropologist Malinowski once wrote: "I should like to put it on record that no honest and sincere Pole would ever have given anything but praise to the political regime of the old Dual Monarchy. Pre-war Austria in its federal constitution presented, in my opinion, a sound solution to all minority problems. It was a model of a miniature League of Nations."[9]

Finally, Berlin's essay on Herder raises a further and even more general puzzle. According to him, Herder holds that, though cultures are "incommensurable," each culture "is what it is, of literally inestimable value in its own society, and consequently to humanity as a whole"; and further, Herder preaches ("no less than his opponent Kant") that "only persons and societies, and almost all of these, are good in themselves – indeed they are all that is good, wholly good, in the world that we know." But why, one asks, are we to think that almost all societies are good in themselves? For whom, apart from God, can a society be said to be "good"? Whom is it imagined as pleasing or benefiting: presumably not another society? Perhaps "humanity as a whole"? But what is this fabulous Leviathan "humanity as a whole"? What do we know about it or what it feels? What organs does it possess for receiving pleasure or benefit?

The truth seems to be that this is looking for "humanity" in the wrong place. Its real home is in the individual and the single exemplar of the human species: the human being whose passion, to use D. H. Lawrence's words, is "to be within himself the whole of mankind." Here it does makes sense to speak of "good" and "goodness"; for goodness concerns individuals only.

From which it follows that "pluralism" is not really a political concept at all: it does not delineate any system of political organization; nor is "a plural society" a meaningful phrase. "Pluralism" is simply the name for the thing that Herder and Isaiah Berlin so admirably do as individuals: that is to say, project themselves into alien ways of thought and feeling, and hold conflicting values in tension in their minds.

Of course, I suppose it could be argued that a society is "good" exactly to the extent that it encourages its citizens to emulate Berlin and Herder and performs such acts of "pluralistic" imagining. But then, by this criterion, there would be nothing much to choose between a liberal democracy, such as Berlin has flourished in, and a benevolent despotism of the kind that produced Herder. As a *political* concept, "pluralism" seems to lead to some awkward conclusions, and it had better be given up.

3
"We," "Us," and "I"

The great error in treating "pluralism" as a political concept, as opposed to a disposition on the part of an individual, is that it entails picturing a society or state as behaving like an enlightened individual – as taking a disinterested and imaginative pleasure, as an enlightened individual might, in the sheer diversity of human cultures. If one reflects on this a little, it must appear there is no reason to expect anything of the kind. Why should a state feel any such pleasure? At the very least it presupposes an intensely paternalist state, incarnated in a benevolent despot, which is hardly what advocates for "pluralism" have in mind. Swedenborg represented heaven as a thoroughly "pluralist" society, divided into as many smaller societies as there are different "goods" (every single angel "being his own good"), and these societies preferring to keep themselves to themselves – "For with their like they are as if with their own and at home, but with others they are as if with strangers and abroad." This, however, worked only because God, from whom all these "goods" derived, was there to run it in his own supremely despotic way.

But that leads at once to a more basic question. What would it mean for a state to "feel," or to possess an imagination, at all? Are not such things purely the perquisite of an individual?

Are we indeed justified in positing anything at all *in general* about the way that states behave? Well, it may be said that states, of whatever complexion, have recognizable ways of dealing with other states. This is sometimes said to resemble the behavior of the "natural man" or savage toward his fellow men, but at least there seems to be a recognized pattern to it: alliances are entered into, border incidents produce official remonstrances, wars are fought according to certain rules, and treaties are signed. But it is not clear that this entitles us to *personify* states.

Now, there are, as we know, a cluster of cherished ideas and metaphors relating to this subject. Thinkers both classical and medieval were prone to liken the state to a human body, with a prince as its head, the people as its limbs, and so forth.

> The kingly-crowned head, the vigilant eye,
> The counsellor heart, the arm our soldier,
> Our steed the leg, the tongue our trumpeter.[1]

Equally, Plato was fond of arguing that the city resembled the soul, for the same three types of activity were to be found in both.

> SOCRATES: Then does it not now follow that the individual will be wise in the same way and by reason of the same element as the city?
> GLAUCON: Surely.
> SOCRATES: And the city will be courageous by reason of the same element and in the same way as the individual is courageous, and both will have all the other elements of virtue in the same way?
> GLAUCON: Inevitably.
> SOCRATES: Then finally, Glaucon, we shall say that a man is just in the manner in which a city is just.
> GLAUCON: That, too, follows inevitably.[2]

Medieval political theorists, again, were fond of envisaging the state as a corporate personality, according to the same legal fiction by which universities and businesses were conceived of as immortal "persons." They also favored the notion of the "body politic," and theorized as to how some part of this "body" could represent the whole. (It is perhaps part of Hobbes's cleverness that we tend for a moment to misread the famous illustration to his *Leviathan*. Instinctively, we tend to assume that all those citizens dotted about Leviathan's body are to be thought of as, "organically," composing him [i.e., the "body politic"]. Whereas in fact, with his crown and scepter [i.e., the state], Leviathan represents all the powers that those citizens have *stripped themselves of* – forever.)

I am using the term "state" in its ordinary sense, as meaning a nation or empire under its political aspect. In this sense, we may say that a human being *possesses* a culture, as he or she possesses a spinal column or a memory; a human being *belongs* to a nation (or empire or tribe); and he or she *may* belong to a state, in the sense of being a state functionary, but more likely will not.

However, it is states not nations that form alliances and go to war. It thus becomes a question – since the majority of individuals do not actually "belong" to the state – in what sense, if any, they can be said to be "expressed" in it, or what is meant by saying that it acts on their "behalf." An extreme view is the one taken by E. M. Forster, who was inclined to think they were *not* expressed in it, in any meaningful way. Near the end of the 1914–18 war, having read Bertrand Russell's *Principles of Social Reconstruction,* he wrote to Russell (28 July 1918): "For a time I thought you would shake me out of my formula – that though of course there is a connection between civilisation and our private desires and impulses and actions, it is a connection as meaningless as that between a word and the letters that make it up. But the formula holds. The war will only end through exhaustion and nausea. All that is good in humanity must be sweated and vomited out together with what is bad." His word here is "civilisation," not "state," but what he says is by no means absurd.

At any rate, in trying to understand the relation of the individual to the state, we are not very likely to pay credence to hoary fancies about the "body politic" or the resemblance between the soul and the city – any more than we would to the "microcosm" idea, according to which the cosmos is "a great animal" or an enlarged man. These fictions exist merely for the purposes of rhetoric, though as such they have no doubt served statesmen and philosophers wonderfully.

So let us turn to the concept of a nation and of "belonging" to a nation. This has been variously interpreted. Conservative thought has tended to be hostile to the idea of the nation as a congeries of atomic individuals, and has envisaged its members as "belonging" via imaginary categories. For some centuries in the Western world the favorite categories were "estates," or "ranks" or "orders." Then in the early nineteenth century, under the pressure of democratic reform, these were supplanted by the category of "class" and "classes." (In Britain it took a threefold form – "upper," "middle," and "working"; though in many minds this scheme existed side-by-side with a rival binary system, "gentleman" versus "nongentleman.")

Hegel attempted to revive the medieval concept of "estates" (*Stande*), devising a threefold system comprising a "substantial" (or agricultural) estate, a "reflecting or formal" (i.e., business) estate, and a "universal" (or bureaucratic) estate; and for him the word "class" was pejorative, suggesting (precisely) the evils that arise when humans are not organized in "estates." This gave Marx, in his early *Contribution to the Critique of Hegel's "Philosophy of Law,"* large opportunities for satire. Hegel's system of "estates," he said, was a most accurate account of things as they were in Prussia, and therefore a most devastating exposé of that dead and spiritless civil society, cut off from all true political life. Soon afterwards, he appropriated the term "class" and constructed an oppositional twofold system, in opposition to Hegel's harmonious triadic one, consisting of "bourgeois" and "proletariat."

"Class" is a cunning scheme and has driven its claws into our consciousness deeply. It is not to be shrugged off, as we would shrug off medieval fancies about the "body politic," and so forth. Nevertheless, it seems to be our long-term duty to try to unthink it; for it can hardly be denied that it is baneful and belongs with other baneful categories like "race." If this can be achieved, the way will be by prolonged introspection

28

and an exploration of all this system's paradoxes, byways, and rhetorical ruses.

But what is puzzling is that, in its preoccupation with these ancient fictions and dubious "communal representations" (to use the language of Durkheim), the world has not paid half so much attention to what is more genuinely mysterious: I mean, the relationship of the individual, not to the state or to the nation, but to the human species. It is proper to call it a mystery, for it something that, one may suppose, no individual can ever be in a position to understand fully. But it is real, in a sense in which those fictions and metaphors are not, and it is something that seems important to explore. Among its elements are the fact that in so many respects, one is the exact replica of every other human; that one possess the entire human potential; that new generations do not merely come into being at fixed intervals, as it might seem to a parent, but at every second; and that with part of one's mind one is conscious of the eternal present of the species, in the sense expressed by Schopenhauer. ("To the eye of a being of incomparably longer life, which at *one* glance comprehended the human race in its whole duration, the constant alternation of birth and death would present itself as a continuous vibration, and accordingly it would not occur to it at all to see in this an ever new arising out of nothing and passing into nothing.") To these should be added the feeling that the individual might be able to innovate in experience on behalf of others; this may perhaps turn out to be no more than a fiction or metaphor, but certainly is a most compelling one.

The advantage, as has already been said, in chapter 2, is that thinking in terms of the human species removes the need to use the word "humanity" to stand for the totality of human beings, living and dead – a purely mathematical entity, about which nothing useful can really be said. One can neither study "humanity" in this sense, nor have a relation with it. Any relation that one could have with it would have to entail the use of the pronouns "we" or "us," and it is hard to get round Sartre's argument in *L'Etre et le néant* that the desire to speak of the human race as "we" or "us" – very characteristic of certain kinds of humanism – is doomed to frustration. Of the two pronouns, "we" has a purely subjective and private significance, representing no more than a momentary truce in the fight-to-the-death between warring subjectivities. "Us" corresponds somewhat more closely to a reality; that is, the reality of being reduced to an object by another's gaze. But for the whole of humanity to become an "us," it would have to suffer the gaze of a "regarding being" who could never be looked at himself. It would, that is to say, require a God; and – God representing "radical absence" – the effort to realize humanity as "us" becomes a Sisyphean and ultimately hopeless task. "The humanist's 'us' – in its form as 'object' – is an ideal impossible of attainment, though each individual nurses the illusory hope of attaining it by progressively enlarging the circle of communities to which he belongs."[3]

For anyone drawn to the idea of humanism, this insistence of Sartre's on the limited reality of the concept "us" (and even more so of "we") is a help and a warning. It is worth remembering that, in Sartre's *La Nausée*, Roquentin's climactic fit of "nausea" is, precisely, brought on by the thought of humanism. He is lunching with his library acquaintance the Autodidact, who tells him how, after the 1914–18 war, he had lost his religious faith, but not his longing for the sensation of fraternity. In the prison camp, and again at mass, he had been able to feel a brotherhood with all men, and now (after a period of terrible loneliness) he has found it once again in Socialist humanism. It is evident, Roquentin realizes, that the Autodidact has got plans to convert him, and he recalls, gloomily, all the humanisms he has encountered in the past. "Alas I have known so many," he later confides to his journal:

The radical humanist is particularly a friend of officialdom. The main preoccupation of the so-called "leftish" humanist is preserving human

*values; be belongs to no party, because he does not want to betray his
precious humanity, but his sympathies go out to the humble; it is to
them he consecrates his fine classical culture. He is usually a widower
with a fine eye, always misted with tears: he weeps on anniversaries.
He also loves cats and dogs and all the superior mammals. The Communist writer has loved men since the second Five-Year Plan: he pun-
ishes because he loves. Modest like all truly strong men, he knows how
to hide his feelings but also how to convey, by a look, an inflection
of the voice, the fierce yet tender brotherly love that lurks behind his
harsh words. The Catholic humanist, the late-comer, the Benjamin,
speaks about men in a tone of wonder. What a beautiful fairy-tale,
he exclaims, is the humblest of lives, the life of a London docker or a
woman boot-mender! He has chosen the humanism of the angels. For
the angels' edification he writes long, sad, beautiful novels, which fre-
quently win the* Prix Femina. [4]

And then, Roquentin reflects, there are so many other kinds,
too – a whole mob of them: the humanist who loves men as
they are and the one who loves them as they ought to be;
the humanist who wants to save men with their approval and
the one who means to do so whether they like it or not; the
humanist who loves men in their life and the one who loves
them in their death; the joyful humanist, always with a joke on
his lips, and the somber humanist, principally met at wakes
and funerals. "They all hate one another – as individuals, that
is to say, not of course as 'men.' But the Autodidact does not
know this: he has taken the whole lot into himself, like cats
in a bag, and they tear out each others' eyes there without his
noticing." The trouble with humanism, Roquentin tells himself with growing horror, is that it can absorb, it can *digest*,
all human attitudes, turning them into the same sticky white
paste. A few moments later, overcome by this vision, he suf-
fers the existential terror that gives Sartre's novel its title.

There is, indeed, an alternative way of saying "we" and "us"
to mankind that may, at first sight, seem to escape the problem posed by Sartre. I mean the liberal-humanist one, which
regards the ambition to say "we" to all mankind as absurd,

almost by definition, and takes it as its aim merely to expand the "we"-group to which one belongs already. I am thinking of an essay in Richard Rorty's *Contingency, Irony and Solidarity*. Rorty argues that what prompted a gentile to hide a Jew from the Nazis during the Second World War was not the recognition of "a core self," a human essence, common to all human beings. The idea of such an "essence," imposing a universal moral claim on all humans, has, he says, done useful rhetorical service in the past; nevertheless it is a fallacy, and the motives prompting philanthropic behavior are always in fact based on exclusion. They affirm a sense of "we" ("our sort of people"), as opposed to "them" (the wrong sort of people). Indeed, says Rorty, quoting Wilfrid Sellers, that is what "morality" consists of: it is a matter of "we-intentions," the core meaning of "immoral action" being "the sort of thing *we* don't do" – it is an expression of "we"-consciousness. Thus, in the given case of Jews in Nazi-occupied countries, the motive of those who helped them would not have been solidarity with the human race as a whole but a feeling that the endangered Jew was somehow "one of us" – a fellow Milanese, a fellow Jutlander, a fellow member of the same union or profession, or the like.

Something is pretty surely not right here. One's instinct is that it does not do justice to those who risked their life on behalf of Jews – justice, not to their bravery, but to their imagination. But in any event, the theory about "we-consciousness" can fairly simply be seen to be a fallacy. We only have to think once again of Huck Finn. There can be no doubt that Huck's white elders would have called helping the negro Jim to escape an "immoral action" and "the sort of thing *we* don't do." Mark Twain's novel is perhaps the most celebrated challenge in all literature to the theory that the "moral law" is merely shorthand for what "what we do, or don't do." Huck Finn subscribes to this theory unreservedly. What "we believe," as he understands it, is that an escaped negro slave must be handed over to the authorities and that anyone who disobeys this rule may very likely go to hell. The only trouble is, he cannot bring himself to do what it prescribes. It is not that he invokes some other "we" to sanction this. It is merely that he, the individual Huck Finn, an "I," finds he cannot do it. Are we to think him a fool?

Rorty goes on to argue that the case of human solidarity is simply one example of the general (pragmatist) principle that – contrary to Kant's teaching – there are no "absolute" moral principles or truths of reason, all moralities being merely contingent historical phenomena. The idea of human solidarity is "simply the fortunate happenstance creation of modern times"; and "The right way to take the slogan 'We have obligations to human beings simply as such' is as a means of reminding ourselves to keep trying to expand our sense of 'us' as far as we can."

But as his argument develops, one sees that it has a radical flaw – and one to do, precisely, with the words "we" and "us." For he goes on to restate his position in the form of a paradox, which seems rather a neat one at first sight. "We" (twentieth-century liberals), he says, are ethnocentric, for we have of necessity to start from "our" (unargued) liberal values; but we are so in a peculiar fashion: for "we" (this particular liberal "we") are ethnocentric in the cause of *abolishing* ethnocentrism: "What takes the curse off this ethnocentrism is not that the largest such group is "humanity" or "all rational beings" – no one, I have been claiming, *can* make *that* identification – but, rather, that it is the ethnocentrism of a "we" ("we liberals") which is dedicated to enlarging itself, to creating an even larger and more variegated *ethnos*. It is the "we" of the people who have been brought up to distrust ethnocentrism."[5]

Now, what is wrong with this is that from Rorty's wording one might think he was making a political statement; and indeed with half his mind that is plainly what he feels he is doing. What other meaning can we attach to the words "a 'we' . . . dedicated to enlarging itself, to creating an even

33

larger and more variegated *ethnos*"? He is evidently talking about a community, in its relations with other communities. Yet who, politically speaking, is this "we" – these "twentieth-century liberals"? Are they a real-life group of people, personally known to one another? If so, where do they meet, how can they be contacted, and what practical steps can we imagine them taking to create an "even larger and more variegated *ethnos*"? Would it be at the local council level, or the national level (in, say, Britain, or France, or the United States), or the international level?

Well, of course, the answer is that the word "we" here is merely a figure of rhetoric, a pulpit "we," as in "We are all sinners." All that is really meant is "I" – that is, Rorty himself, who earnestly wishes that a larger proportion of the globe's inhabitants would regard one another as "we" rather than as "they." It is a desire one fervently goes along with. Though what his language does not convey, and perhaps should have done, is that, judging from Bosnia or India or various parts of Africa and the Middle East, the proportion is actually at the moment not increasing but fast shrinking – the principle of insurgent nationalism, religious fundamentalism, and regional separatism being, precisely, to contract the area within which one will say "we." This should be a worrying thought for a liberal. Anyway, what Rorty is voicing is just a wish, a sentiment, an expression of his own inner freedom from enthnocentrism. It has no political content.

On the other hand, objections to the "monadic" idea of the human species, according to which the entire potentiality of the species is reproduced in every individual, have always been strongly political. We may think, for instance, of Aristotle. The way that Aristotle talks about the human species, in the opening pages of the *Politics,* is bound to jar fearfully on almost any post-Kantian reader. Here he is on the slave-master relationship: "He that can by his intelligence foresee things needed is by nature ruler and master, while he whose bodily

34

strength enables him to perform them is by nature a slave, one of those who are ruled." Or again: "Property is an instrument to living; an estate is a multitude of instruments; so a slave is an animated instrument." Or this on women: "Nature has distinguished between female and slave. She recognizes different functions and lavishly provides different tools, not an all-purpose tool like the Delphic knife. Every instrument will perform its work best when it is made to serve not many purposes but *one*. So it is with the different functions of female and slave. Some non-Greek communities fail to understand this and assign to female and slave exactly the same status. This is because they have no section of the community which is by nature fitted to rule and command."

Aristotle, as this remark about "different tools" shows, was by conviction a splitter-up of the human species, and certainly one who saw no sin in regarding human beings as means and not ends. He was also a "division-of-labor" man – almost as much so as Plato, who regarded the division of labor as a model of Justice itself. ("There was an image of justice," Socrates is made to say to Glaucon in *Republic*, "in the principle that he whom nature intended for a shoemaker should attend to shoemaking and nothing else, and that the carpenter should do carpentry, and so on.") By comparison with their attitude, which is as it were a sketch for Hindu caste theory, it is curious how much respect Adam Smith, the supreme apologist for the division of labor, pays to the concept of an undivided human nature:

The difference of natural talents is, in reality, much less than we are aware of; and the very different genius which appears to distinguish men of different professions, when grown up to maturity, is not upon many occasions so much the cause as the effect of the division of labour. The difference between the most dissimilar characters, between a philosopher and a common street porter, for example, seems to arise not so much from nature as from habit, custom, and education. When they came into the world, and for the first six or eight years of their exis-

35

tence, they were perhaps very much alike, and neither their parents nor play-fellows could perceive any remarkable difference.

Aristotle, you might say, was the ancestor of Kipling, whose constant preoccupation was to split up the human psyche and to regard the world solely in terms of species or "kinds" or "breeds." According to the Kipling view, you were to belong to the species Woman, or Irishman, or Saxon, or "oriental" or *babu;* this was to be your "kind." But further, according to this new version of classical ethics, though you might be compelled (in the civilized world, just as in the jungle) to co-operate with other "kinds," it was your deepest wish to live only with your own. This schismatic and zoological worldview of Kipling's precluded not only the Brotherhood of Man (a favorite butt with him) but human innovation – assuming as it did that people will only be capable of doing what it is in their "kind" to do.

We can contrast such splitting-up of the human species with the D. H. Lawrence doctrine, that "the ultimate passion of every man is to be within himself the whole of mankind." Lawrence attached importance to the theory and voiced it again in a letter to Gordon Campbell (3 March 1915): "It is not that I care about *other people:* I know that *I* am the English nation – that *I* am the European race. . . . *L'Etat c'est moi.* It is a great saying, and should be true of every man." The thought, in various versions, runs through a lot of Lawrence and is often recurring in *The Rainbow* and *Women in Love.* In the night scene in the chapter "Moony" in *Women in Love,* Ursula, sitting on the bank of Willey Water, becomes aware that Birkin is near at hand but unconscious of her presence. "Supposing he did something he would not wish to be seen doing, thinking he was quite private," she reflects? "But there, what did it matter? How could it matter, what he did? How can there be any secrets, we are all the same organisms? How can there be any secrecy, when everything is known to all of us?" The thought has its logical place in Lawrence's philosophy, as expounded in *The Crown,* and relates to his belief that we may have all the great experiences and visions, on condition that we do not try to cling to them.

What enters into the conception is that one can experience things on behalf of others. The idea is evoked touchingly, in a purely personal context, in the lovely poem "Everlasting Flowers for a Dead Mother," where Lawrence imagines his dead mother looking out on the Italian scene through his eyes.

> All the things that are lovely —
> The things you never knew —
> I wanted to gather them one by one
> And bring them to you.
>
> But never now, my darling,
> Can I gather the mountain-tips
> From the twilight like half-shut lilies
> To hold to your lips.
>
> And never the two-winged vessel
> That sleeps below in the lake
> Can I catch like a moth between my hands
> For you to take.
>
> But hush, I am not regretting:
> It is far more perfect now.
> I'll whisper the ghostly truth to you
> And tell you how
>
> I know you here in the darkness,
> How you sit in the throne of my eyes
> At peace, and look out of the windows
> In glad surprise.

In *The Rainbow* and *Women in Love* the thought is extended to generations. By the repetitional pattern in these novels it is suggested that one generation can innovate in experience on behalf of another.

We are in a realm of thought here that is certainly mystical but may not have to be termed vague. At all events, others are drawn to it with equal force from their own very different angles. It is what the young Stephen Dedalus is invoking, grandiloquently, at the end of Joyce's *Portrait of the Artist:* "Welcome, O life! I go to encounter for the millionth time the reality of experience and to forge in the smithy of my soul the uncreated conscience of my race." From the context, it is plain that Stephen is speaking not just of the Irish "race" but of the human race or species in general. The idea of innovation or "forging" on behalf of others has to be balanced by the idea of repetition and recurrence, in the Vico sense (he is to do it "for the millionth time") – and of course, no doubt, some joke about *forgery* is also lurking. Nevertheless, Stephen is explicit, and Joyce himself not much less so, about the possibility – not merely metaphorical but actual – of innovating on behalf of the human species.

The error of "humanisms" in the past, as has been said, has been its way of conceiving of "humanity" as a totality, a collection of human beings, instead of as a species replicated entire in every individual. The distinction was important to Marx, who spoke tenderly of man's "species-being" and called communism a "humanism," by which he meant an effort to reclaim this species-being from its present estrangement and alienation. Communism was, he said, "the complete return of man to himself as a *social* (i.e., human) being – a return accomplished consciously and embracing the entire wealth of previous development."

The point has a bearing on historiography. For, however convincingly historians tell the story of the world, one is aware that something is wrong or missing. It is a story not like other stories, of the kind we are familiar with in fables or novels, since from moment to moment the occupants of roles die off and are replaced by a new set. Historical narrative has no way of expressing this all-important fact of birth and reproduction – that is to say, the need for traditions and images of the past and of things as they are to be created over and over again in the minds of the newly born. (We soften the force of this fact by talking of "generations," but the truth is, new generations begin, not at twenty-five-year intervals, but every instant.)

In some people, this causes, very naturally, a resistance to history, with its insistence on sequence. Walt Whitman, though under the shadow of a great historical event, the American Civil War, writes in "Song of Myself":

> I have heard what the talkers were talking, the talk of
>   the beginning and the end,
> But I do not talk of the beginning or the end.
>
> There never was any more inception than there is now,
> Nor any more youth or age than there is now,
> And will never be any more perfection than there is now,
> Nor any more heaven and hell than there is now.

The lines, moreover, come in a poem that begins in thoroughly "monadic" fashion, admitting no distinction between "humanity" and the individual self:

> I celebrate myself, and sing myself,
> And what I assume you shall assume,
> For every atom belonging to me as good belongs to you.

D. H. Lawrence, it must be admitted, will not let Whitman get away with this. "Walter, leave off," he tells him. "You are not HE. You are just a limited Walter." [6] (This reminds one that the "monad" idea was only half of Lawrence's message, the other half saying: "The living self has one purpose only: to come into the fulness of its own being.")

A resistance to history can, of course, go even further. For Schopenhauer, the "philosophy of history" in Hegel's sense – the story of a collection of human beings moving toward a goal – was a "crude and positivistic" error. What history narrated was only "the long, heavy, and confused dream of humanity" and was hardly deserving of serious study. All human reality, according to Schopenhauer, pertains to the *species,* and the species represents a perpetual present – not the drops of the waterfall but the unshaken rainbow above it.

What is plain is that Schopenhauer's conception of history and "humanity," like its opposite, destroys the basis for humanism, anyway of the kind I am groping toward. Humanism requires that history be taken seriously – only with a proviso, that the relation of the individual to history is not a straightforward affair and has to accommodate a paradox, that the proper ambition of any human is to be within himself or herself the whole of humankind. But once this is granted, it seems to be the most effective way to study human affairs. To study "humanity" seems to require two things. It calls for the examination of diverse cultures, and it calls for introspection (i.e., meditating on oneself as an exemplar of the human race); and these are part of the same mental act, a matter of asking, "What would it be *like* (for oneself) to be so-and-so?"

But the same is true of the attempt to change humanity. For only a human being who regards himself or herself as containing the whole human potential and as able, by introspection, to picture what it might be "like" (for oneself) to be something quite different from what one happens to be, is in a position to think through false and harmful distinctions of race, class, and gender – as a prelude to *un*thinking them. If it seems, moreover, that I attach too much value to introspection, I would point to one overwhelmingly important brand of "race" thinking: I mean anti-Semitism. For the secret of anti-Semitism is that it lurks there, as a pattern of thought or superstition, in the mind of even the most humane and liberal-minded European, non-Jewish and Jewish alike. The only hope of eradicating it finally is by the approach Sartre adopted in his "Portrait of an Anti-Semite": that is to say by thinking these thoughts through, in their insane logic, to the end – which is to say recognizing them as *one's own*.

4
Race and Nationalism

I have argued in another book that the right way to study social "class" is by introspection, and that it is by this method that the real hope lies of getting rid of the concept. For "class," a mode of classifying without legal basis, does not exist "out there," in the visible world, but within the human mind and bosom, and it is only there that it can be properly observed.[1]

The same seems to be true of the much simpler concept of "race." If I ask myself how I define myself racially, I find myself utterly at a loss. Am I, for instance, an "Anglo-Saxon," a "Teuton," a "Celt," an "Aryan," or a "Caucasian"? No, I don't really feel myself any of those things, and anyway how would I know if I were?

But perhaps I should consider the matter more biologically? Shall I, for instance, look for my place in J. Deniker's anthropological classification, which is principally based on hair? This would put me either in his category D ("Fair, wavy or straight hair, light eyes"), of the subdivision Northern European ("rather wavy reddish blonde hair, tall stature, dolicephaly"), or perhaps in his category C ("Wavy brown or black hair, dark eyes"), of the subdivision Western European ("short stature, marked brachycephaly, round face").

Now, if I *were* to describe myself as, say, a Celt or perhaps a Teuton, as people were so fond of doing in the nineteenth century, it would entail other beliefs about myself, too. For instance, maybe, that I was subject to "the blind hysterics of the Celt" (Tennyson), or that "in my love of women there was little of the Teutonic depths and earnestness" (J. R. Green).

By contrast, even if Deniker were able to locate me in his system (as no doubt he could have done – though awkwardly I am of medium height, with a longish face, and have, or used to have, straight brown hair), it would seem to be more his affair than mine. After all, from my hair and cranial index, he is not going to start drawing inferences about my character. To put the point very simply: for the purposes of such a system as his, the texture of my hair or the shape of my skull are not *indications* of my race, they *are* my race. At least, this would be a perfectly viable system and is, no doubt, all that many biological taxonomists would claim for their work.

It is always possible of course that, from my hair and skull, an anthropologist will start drawing inferences about the migrations of my ancestors. But even a layman can see why this is an error and why such theories can never be more than conjectural and unscientific. For presumably a racial "type" (i.e., a subdivision within the species *Homo sapiens*) ought to be the equivalent of a "variety" in botany (shall we say, the variety *Narcissus pseudonarcissus moschatus* of the species *Narcissus pseudonarcissus*). But the botanical parallel does not actually work – for the very good reason that, unlike botanical varieties, human beings interbreed. Because of this fact, human "types" must be in continual change, and moreover have presumably always been so, it being a fallacy to posit some primordial set of genetically "pure" prototypes later subjected to mongrelization. It follows that any attempt, by inference from the hair and skulls and so on of the living, to write *history* is bound to be more or less vain. To distinguish the past effects of migration from those of local interbreeding, climate, and natural selection can only be done by reckless conjecture, and in this respect anthropology cannot be an exact science like its ally philology.

It is for some such reason that, as most writers on the subject freely admit, biological anthropology – unlike botany and zoology – is a perfect chaos of rival classifications. J. C. Trevor, in his article "Race" in *Chambers' Encyclopaedia*, says that "no

universal agreement as to the number of validity of *taxa* exists,"
and he gives some details of Deniker's classification of 1889,
the utterly different one of A. C. Haddon of 1909, and Duckworth's classification of 1904 (which envisages seven human
groups based on the cephalic index, prognathism, and cranial capacity), before outlining his own fivefold system of
Mongoliforms, Negriforms, Europiforms, Khoisaniforms, and
Australiforms, with their respective subdivisions. But then, as
one reflects, there is no strong reason why things should be
otherwise. For, after all, there is no limit to the number of
ways in which one might classify human beings, any more than
any other collection of items – say, the contents of one's desk
or the books in one's library. It all depends on what you want
from your classification and your ability to carry it through
with consistency. (Thus, when Trevor praises Duckworth's
classification as "one of the most objective approaches to a
'natural' system yet formulated," he seems to be falling into a
favorite delusion of taxonomists: that there is a "natural" classification, if only one could find it.)

The point I am getting at is that "race" is not a word, like
"species," with an agreed technical meaning, and anthropologists are not much more consistent in their usage of it than
the rest of us. As a word, it is more or less of a blank check,
to be filled in in whatever way the speaker chooses. Thus one
will hear of the "human race," the "Irish race," a "White" and
a "Black" race, the "Semitic" race, the "Teutonic" race, and
so on – a quite unsystematic jumble of meanings. Further,
we should not suppose that racial terms like Celt or Teuton
or Aryan, absurd as we are likely to think them nowadays,
are any *more* absurd, or more intellectually disreputable, than
the terms Magyar or Slav. None of these terms will bear any
kind of serious scrutiny in thinking about the modern world.
(When E. H. Minns writes that "the physical type of the Slavs
is not sufficiently clear to help in throwing light upon the past
of the race," one is aware of a non sequitur; one wants to ask
what, in that case, justifies his talking about "the Slavs.")[2]

As we know, these theories about race flourished exceedingly in the nineteenth century, especially among historians and novelists, and also in the first chapters of biographies, where the author aired theories about the subject's "blood." In retrospect, and after the Nazi era, one feels too much indulgence was shown to them. It was (still is, among some people) the convention to find it amusing, even "brilliant," to make a remark like the young Guizot's: that the French Revolution was a "*revanche* of the Gallo-Romans." Readers took it in their stride when Balzac invoked the "tenacity" of the Breton race; and the engaging qualities of the "Irish race" brought them much patting of the head in fiction and journalism, as well as sage doubts as to how well they would cope in the industrial age. The Edwardian "Home-Ruler" J. M. Robertson believed these "charming" fantasies about race were in fact a major factor in the tragic mess made of the Irish question, and his book *The Saxon and the Celt* is a rich anthology of race nonsense. Here, as quoted by him, is the historian Amédée Thierry's *Histoire des Gaulois* (1828):

> The salient traits of the Gaulish family, those which most differentiate it, in my opinion, from the other human families, may be thus summarised: a personal bravery which is not equalled among the ancient peoples; a frank and impetuous spirit, open to all impressions, eminently intelligent; but along with that an extreme mobility, no constancy, a marked repugnance to the ideas of discipline and order prevailing among the Germanic races, great ostentation, in fine, a perpetual disunion, the fruit of excessive vanity. If one should summarily compare the Gaulish family with that Germanic family which we have just named, one might say that the personal sentiment, the individual me, is too much developed with the first, and that with the other it is not enough.

Or again, this from Nott and Gliddon's *Types of Mankind* (Philadelphia, 1854): "*Dark*-skinned races, history attests, are fit only for military governments. It is the unique rule genial to their physical nature; they are unhappy without it, even now, at

44

Paris. None but the fair-skinned types of mankind have been able to realise, in peaceful practice, the old Germanic system described by Tacitus – '*De minoribus rebus principes consultant; de majoribus, omnes*' [About minor matters, the leaders confer; about major ones, everybody]."

When reading about Pan-Slavism in the nineteenth century, and the famous Pan-Slav congress that met in Prague in 1848, what dominates one's mind is not so much the wild "scatter" of messianic visions and political manoeuvres as the impossibility, by the time of the nineteenth century, of attaching any definite meaning to the term "Slav." (But this, of course, was exactly what constituted its charm.) The name was first recorded in the sixth century A.D., as relating to a people living somewhere around the Carpathians, and efforts have been made in some quarters, much pooh-poohed in other quarters, to relate this people to the Scythians of the ancient world. At all events, a sketchy history can be made out for these "Slavs" or "Sclaves" in the early Middle Ages. Also, there is a large group of languages that it has been found convenient to label Slavonic. But, the point is, what had the nineteenth century to do with this wildly archaic term "Slav," any more than with "Anglo-Saxon" or "Pict"? The answer is plain: it was to milk it for all it was worth, in the knowledge that the claim that one is a Slav is not very likely to be challenged (for on what grounds would anyone challenge it?), which leaves it open to one to lay claim to various inspiring "Slav" characteristics. Though indeed even this rule was liable to get broken. The Polish Pan-Slavists of the 1840s found themselves in the difficulty that their very purpose in "calling to life" the Slavonic peoples was to form a "bulwark against the barbarians of the North" – that is to say, against the Russians, who are usually supposed to be Slavs. They solved it by deciding that the Russians were really not Slavs at all but "Mongols."

NATIONALISM

If it is agreed, then, that race is an entirely empty and spurious concept, we need to think about its relations with the

45

term "nation," which, by contrast, denotes an idea we need and can hardly get along without. Needless to say, people talk endless rubbish about "national characteristics," and novelists and others have often made their living by it. It is a sort of weak spot even with historians. They conduct themselves for most of the time with professional objectivity, not indulging in hindsight or teleology, and then something in what they are studying strikes a chord in their breast, reminding them perhaps of their favorite novels, and they become quite ahistorical, murmuring dreamily about "the English gift for compromise" or the characteristics of "the English mind." Even so sensible a man as George Orwell fell into the trap, claiming that "a profound, almost unconscious patriotism and an inability to think logically are the abiding features of the English character, traceable in English literature from Shakespeare downwards." (The profound patriotism of Shelley and Byron? The incapacity for logical thought of Lewis Carroll and J. S. Mill? It won't do; Orwell for once is maundering.)

Nevertheless there are perfectly serious things to be said about "Englishness" and "Frenchness," that is to say about the cultural traditions and ways of doings things peculiar to France and to England, and without getting deep into *Volksgeist* or indulging in the idea that "the French" or "the English" have a corporate personality. It also makes sense to *love* France or England. It even makes sense to frame a remark like "Algeria was never a nation before the revolution": the point may be undecidable, but the remark itself is not meaningless. Where the concept of a "nation" begins to grow really false, and moreover dangerous, is at the point where it appeals to the concept of "race."

Admittedly, postmodernist theorists, of the Homi Bhabha school, are inclined to debunk the concept of nations and nationalism as a mere "myth of origin," an illegitimate "totalization" or piece of "essentialism." For nationalism, Homi Bhabha would wish to substitute a locating of oneself in "in-between spaces," an "interstitial" passage between fixed identifications [that] opened up "the possibility of a cultural hybridity that entertains difference without an assumed or imposed hierarchy."[3] But, as sometimes with radical feminism, it is not really clear whether what is at stake is a communal identity or merely a personal one; and at all events, what is being prescribed is political "pluralism" under a new disguise, with the wishfulness and utopianism that always comes with it.

More teasingly, Frederic Jameson, in an article "Third World Literature in the Era of Multinational Capitalism,"[4] has argued that, whereas American intellectuals have outgrown the concept of national "identity," as part of a general rejection of the "centered subject" and "the old unified ego of bourgeois individualism," it is still an absolute necessity in the Third World – Third World intellectuals being, and rightly, obsessed with "us" and what "we" have to do and "what we can't do and what we do better than this or that nationality." Indeed Jameson goes further. He lays it down that all Third World literature is bound to (it "cannot but") take the form of national allegory.

Against this, Aijaz Ahmad has asked, very reasonably, what possible sense it can make to lump together, shall we say, Achebe, Borges, Naipaul, and Lu Xun as something called "Third World Literature."[5] To which one must add the question, how could anyone have ever regarded the term "the Third World" itself as a theoretical entity, or as more than the merest journalistic mnemonic? At all events, the term, and the three-worlds theory in general, ought now to be safely defunct, since there is no longer a Second World, the Socialist bloc having vanished from the scene. But, weirdly, the term "the Third World" is still in use.

But a further objection to Jameson also suggests itself, one more directly relevant to this book. For in his rule that Third World literature "cannot but" take the form of national allegory, one seems to hear the classic accents of dictatorial philanthropy. Third World intellectuals, it seems to be saying, cannot hope to behave like *us,* and it wouldn't be good for

47

them if they did; and really, by comparison with them, we post-modernists are a terribly effete and self-indulgent lot. ("The luxury of the Sartrean blink offers a welcome escape from the 'nightmare of history,' but at the same time it condemns our culture to psychologism and the 'projections' of private subjectivity.") The perversity of this can be seen easily enough if one imagines that one were, oneself, a young Nigerian or Chilean, or Indonesian or Indian writer. As such one would naturally, and very properly, assume that, being an exemplar of the human species, one might write *anything*. A critic might come along afterwards and show that our work had been "determined" by our historical situation – that would be his privilege, and what he got paid for – but it is not for him to say beforehand what it has been determined we shall write.

Nationalism and nation forming is of passionate concern to us at present, with the break-up of the Soviet Union, and I am inclined to think that Ernest Gellner made more sense on the subject than anyone before. (Benedict Anderson, in *Imagined Communities* [1983], corrects and enlarges him at various points but seems in general to go along with him.) So let me briefly sketch Gellner's theory. According to this, nationalism is essentially a product of the industrial age. Industrial society, unlike any type of society hitherto known, lives by sustained and perpetual growth, and for this reason it requires universal literacy. Literacy, once the speciality of a clerisy, has to be extended to all citizens, and there is a need for an all-purpose or "generic" type of education, enabling citizens to move from one occupation to another without too much difficulty. In a word, an industrial society requires homogeneity. It has to renounce or abolish self-reproducing kinship groups and hereditary specializations and train the population at large for the administrative tasks once reserved for a special class of "Mamluks." In agrarian societies, people's allegiances are both narrower and wider than the polity, but in industrial society (only the state having the resources to maintain universal education) "high culture" and the polity have to coincide. "Modern man is not loyal to a monarch or a land or a faith, whatever he may say, but to a culture," and this identity of high culture and polity is the secret of nationalism.

One is, next, to consider the losers in the original race to industrialization: those illiterate and half-starved populations, "sucked from their erstwhile rural cultural ghettoes into the melting pots of shanty-towns," who, for reasons of language, culture, and so on, find themselves at the bottom of the pile. For them – given that the universal trend is now toward nationalism – the answer often seemed to be to form, or to join, a separate nation, a process that would probably involve inventing traditions, reviving dead languages, and creating folk heroes.

Gellner invents an imaginary scenario for the evolution of a nationalism. The "Ruritanians" are a peasant population speaking a group of related dialects, which only they speak – the nobility and officialdom employing a quite different court language, and the clergy and the (much-disliked) petty traders using different tongues again.[6]

In the past, the Ruritanian peasants had had many griefs, "movingly and beautifully recorded in their lament-songs (painstakingly collected by village schoolmasters late in the nineteenth century, and made well known to the international musical public by the compositions of the great Ruritanian national composer L.)." The pitiful oppression they suffered provoked, in the eighteenth century, the guerrilla resistance led by the famous Ruritanian social bandit K., whose deeds are said still to persist in the folk memory, not to mention several novels and two films. Honesty compels the admission, however, that K. was captured by his own compatriots, and that it was a compatriot who presided over the tribunal that condemned him to a painful death. Moreover, the folk songs, "now incorporated in the repertoire of the Ruritanian youth, camping and sports movement," do not disclose much evidence of serious discontent on the part of the peasantry with their linguistic and cultural situation, "however grieved they were by other, more earthy matters."

In all this, Gellner insists (and it takes the sting out of his irony) that the nationalists did not know what they were doing, any more than the creators of the industrial revolution knew what they were doing; they were guided by forces outside their own awareness. Thus no doubt it was in good faith that they pictured themselves as dispossessed heirs of a historic nation; it is merely that they were deceived. Nationalism is not what it seems, and above all it is not what it seems to itself. It is *not* (as Hegel liked to imagine it) "the awakening of an old, latent, dormant force"; it is not the natural and universal form of political life, nor do nations constitute "a political version of the doctrine of natural kinds."

On the other hand, according to this view, nationalism, as a political form appropriate to the industrial age, is here to stay. Its critics, who represent it as an arbitrary whim, a poison with which meddling ideologues infect the bloodstream of otherwise viable communities, are mistaken. The "cultural shreds and patches" used by nationalists may be arbitrary inventions, and it could be that others would have served just as well. (In more recent days, nonwhiteness and fundamentalist religion have figured largely in nation forming.) But there is nothing contingent and accidental about the *principle* of nationalism. It is nationalism that engenders nations, not the other way round; and the principle of nationalism is deeply rooted in the conditions in which most of us now live.

Let us for a moment go along with this theory of Gellner's – anyway as regards the first wave of modern nationalisms, which is all I have so far discussed. It certainly has the virtue of clarity. But indeed, helped by Gellner, we can do a little further clearing of our mind. He says that "agrarian man" can be compared to a natural species, which is able to survive in the natural environment, whereas "industrial man" can survive only in specially bounded and constructed units – "a kind of giant aquarium or breathing chamber" – maintained by a national educational and communications system. He continues: "It would not in principle be impossible to have a single such cultural/educational goldfish bowl for the entire globe, sustained by a single political authority and a single educational system."

It is a startling remark, reinforcing one's impression that Gellner slightly underestimates (of course he does not altogether ignore) the role of *territory* in the concept of a "nation." It is hard to imagine a nation that possessed no frontiers, if only on the principle of the reverend Mr. Sorley in *A Passage to India:* "We must exclude someone from our gathering, or we shall be left with nothing." But at all events, Gellner is plainly asking us to regard even this global community as a "nation" and not as any sort of supranational entity.

Here one feels he is in the right, at least in the light of his general theory. But indeed, with all respect to Kant and others, there seems much to be said for regarding a supranational community as a rather fruitless concept. For this reason: the social systems we hear most about, like the "nation" or feudalism or the Greek city-state, did not come into being because somebody decided they were a good idea. They came about blindly, as the result of external causes, a vast complication of them – economic, climatic, demographic, medical, and religious. It is only by reflecting on a situation they have already long been in that occupants of such a system, or their philosophers, begin to decide what its theory is – or even what to call it. (The name "feudalism," as denoting a kind of society, seems first to have been used in 1727.)

Now, it is always possible that, one day, humankind will wake up to find itself in a "world order" or supranational state, though the idea offers large logical difficulties. But, at least, it has not done so up to now; and the existence of international institutions, for instance the United Nations or the International Court of Justice, should not be seen as a step in that direction, since they presuppose nations. It is of course easy to have fantasies about these matters. William of Ockham held that the world-state already existed and that, by a formal sentence of the "Corporation of All Mortal Men," whole portions of mankind could be deprived of their active rights in it, as a penalty for their corporate misdeeds. (It had happened to the Jews and heathens, causing their share in the empire to devolve to the Christians.)

The better course, though, seems to be to leave the "world order" to the schoolmen and to science fiction and try to make the best one can of the nation-state. What the political theorists of the European Community want, though they do not always talk that way, can only be to create a new large *nation*, a nation prosperous and powerful enough to hold its own against the United States. This is a meaningful aim, whether one approves of it or thinks it feasible or not, and it is the most usual aim for a federation.

The "nation," then – a meaningful enough concept if one interprets it rightly – is beset by several phantoms: the ineffectual phantoms of the "world-state" and of "pluralism," and the exceedingly effective and baneful phantom, "race." All the ills of which nationalism has been accused, for instance during the Bosnian conflict of 1993, would be better blamed on "race" – that almost entirely empty concept, so easily invoked to support almost any kind of aggression.

A PROBLEM FOR HISTORIOGRAPHY

But it will be asked, how can a historian – however much he or she may dislike or distrust "race" terminology – get on without using it? The question is raised very strikingly by a book, Noel Malcolm's *Bosnia: A Short History,* which deals with the Bosnian war. For Malcolm repeatedly insists, indeed he makes it almost his central theme, that the identities of the participants in the war – whether we think of these as racial, national, or religious – were, more often than not, of their own choosing. At the first Communist Party Congress in Yugoslavia after the Second World War, it was stated that "Bosnia cannot be divided between Serbia and Croatia, not only because

Serbs and Croats live mixed together on the whole territory, but also because the territory is inhabited by Muslims who have not yet decided on their national identity." What "decided on their national identity" meant here, says Malcolm, was "decided whether to call themselves Serb or Croats."[7] In the 1948 census, however, it was envisaged that some Bosnians might want to describe themselves as "Muslims," and these were given three options: they could call themselves Muslim Serbs, Muslim Croats or "Muslims, nationally undeclared" (or "undetermined"). Finally, on the census form in 1971 there appeared, as an option, the description "Muslim, in the sense of a nation."

In a word, what one called oneself in post–World War II Yugoslavia was, as it still is, essentially a political act, a matter of political expediency, and Malcolm is much to be praised for bringing this out so vividly. But the problem is, in the very next paragraph he will be narrating what the "Serbs," the "Croats," and "Muslims" (not to mention "Bosnians") in Bosnia did, as if these appellations were in no way problematic. Nor is it obvious how he could do otherwise. This is not just a trivial or technical problem: on the contrary, it seems to raise profound doubts about what "history," in the conventional style practiced by Malcolm, is or can be doing.

But evidently he does not see it in this light himself. His is in many ways a humane and intelligent book, but he is capable of writing such a passage as the following: "In the case of a Macedonian Slav Muslim, it is possible to talk about religion as a kind of surface layer which can be peeled back to reveal the ethnic or national substratum underneath. Remove the layer of Islam, and you are left with a Slav who can be identified as 'Macedonian' by criteria of language and history."[8] This, with its tacit claim that one can say what such a "Macedonian Slav Muslim" *really* is, seems an intolerable kind of discourse, in which nothing true could ever be said, all its terms – "Slav," "Muslim," "Macedonian," "identified," "criteria," "substratum," and "ethnic" – being equally question begging.

It remains to deal with a feature of many of the texts I have been quoting, and that seems to need a closer look: I mean the term "ethnic." The leading definition of *ethnic* in the OED is "pertaining to race" (an *ethnographer* being "one who treats descriptively of the races of mankind"). Nevertheless, it is precisely to avoid the word "race" that this term "ethnic" (and "ethnic group") is more and more resorted to. In *We Europeans,* Julian Huxley and A. C. Haddon wrote: "Nowhere does a human group now exist which corresponds closely to a systematic sub-species in animals, since various original sub-species have crossed repeatedly and constantly. For existing populations the non-committal term *ethnic group* should be used."[9] Their advice has certainly been taken. People resort to the word sometimes to avoid being called "racist," and sometimes also for the good reason given by Huxley and Haddon; that is to say that, in the zoological sense, there *are* no human "races," no human sub-species.

It will be seen, though, how much scope this term gives to bad faith. For to call some conflict or rivalry "ethnic" lends it a kind of spurious authority or justification. It implies, when people decide they cannot get on with others, that what is at stake is not real-life motives, like opportunism, fear, religious prejudice, or insurgent nationalism, but some genetic barrier, some insuperable incompatibility of "blood." It is suggestive that the sole definition of "Ethnick" in Johnson's *Dictionary* is "Heathen; pagan; not Jewish; not Christian" and that the cognate Greek word, as used in the Septuagint, means literally "the nations," with the implication "the non-Jewish nations." Thus the word "ethnic" may be said, historically, to carry a negative connotation: "*Not* Jewish," "*Not* Christian." The word is essentially designed to denote, not so much the intrinsic qualities of a human group – for here the terms "culture" and "culture-group" are more useful and precise – but the phenomenon of one group, for whatever reason, refusing to get on with another. Some of the horror of the phrase "ethnic cleansing," used in the Bosnian conflict, attaches to the word "ethnic" as well as to the word "cleansing."

5
Behalf

I f the idea can be accepted that a human being can experience, and innovate in experience, on behalf of others, it proves a help when considering the general question: what does it mean to do something on someone else's "behalf," and what does it entail? The answer is not absolutely obvious.

A look at the dictionary tells us that the term "behalf" derives from "half," meaning "side," so that "on behalf" originally meant "on the side of," usually referring to one's *own* side. In time, it also came to refer to agency (a master being made legally responsible for actions performed by his servant "on his behalf"). At some point, however, there developed a distinction between the phrases "on behalf of" and "in behalf of," the latter signifying "in the interest of." It is at this point that the term "behalf," by a sort of contradiction, began a close association with altruism and philanthropy.

Let us, then, think about "behalf" in regard to the political life. There must, it seems plain, be an enormous difference between politics on behalf of a group one does not belong to and politics on behalf of a group to which one does. One is tempted to call these "politics on behalf of others" and "politics on one's own behalf," though this would not be exact, since there is also a third possibility, "politics of the person" – the type conventionally regarded as born after the Paris "events" of May 1968.

Victorian Britain, as one need not say, offers many explicit examples of politics of the first kind – that is to say, on behalf of a group that is not one's own: for instance, movements like "Young England" and Christian Socialism. Such a movement sometimes appealed to a medieval-revival chivalry. ("What, after all, could be more chivalrous," writes Mark Girouard in *Return to Camelot,* "than for a gentleman to disregard his own self-interest and the interests of his class, and fight for the rights of working men?")[1] Equally, like utilitarianism, it might draw its inspiration from "science" and "progress." James Mill, writing to Francis Place about his plan to live in France, said that on his and his family's return "we shall, at any rate, have plenty of *knowledge* [italics mine], the habit of living upon little, and a passion for the improvement of the condition of mankind."[2] Harold Perkin, in his *The Origins of Modern English Society 1780–1880,* has trouble in fitting such philanthropists and altruists into his scheme of "classes," since in his scheme the "middle class" is also the acquisitive and entrepreneurial one. He therefore dubs them as the "cranks" and the "forgotten" middle class.[3] There is some intended irony in this; all the same, it is an odd way of describing figures so conspicuous on the British political scene.

But then, perhaps more significantly, some conception of the kind I am speaking of underlay British political life in general and was the rationale for the career of, shall we say, a Lord Shaftesbury or Gladstone or Lord Cecil or Sidney Webb. On the whole, despite the O'Connells and Tom Manns, British parliamentary democracy of the nineteenth-century sort was run, ostensibly anyway, on the assumption that it was honorable to make a career in politics only if it were on behalf of others – people with whom you might have practically nothing in common save a shared humanity. (Things were different with noncareer politicians, and it was considered decent and proper that, in the House of Lords, there should be a few Lord Emsworths representing their own interest, the so-called landed interest – with the saving clause that they were, in some sense, "the nation.")

Now, the psychology of being a politician on this pattern must differ greatly from being one on behalf of a group of which one oneself is a member. It might be a very good thing, psychologically and morally, to devote one's whole life to the interests of some oppressed group of which one was not a member, and yet not be a good thing on the part of someone who *was* a member of it. For the latter, whose personal interests are directly involved, there is an obvious human danger that it may lead to obsession and paranoia. That person will also be exposed to special temptations to corruption or betrayal, or anyway have a special liability to be accused of them. Anyway, appeals to concepts like "injustice" or "moral outrage" really sound better when made on behalf of people whose interests have no connection with one's own. On the lips of the actual victims they are bound to have a hollower ring.

Indeed, it is a matter not merely of psychology but of logic. "Justice," I need not say, is a concept of fundamental importance, but it is the domain, not so much of the victim of injustice, as of the philanthropic outsider. The point comes home to one rather vividly if one thinks of feminism. Early feminists, in their dispute with men, were inclined to appeal to social "justice," but – as later feminists have realized – this was entirely anomalous and illogical. For in the world of actuality, an appeal for justice is an appeal to authority; it presupposes a judge; and who, in this particular case, is to be imagined as the judge? It could, of course, be God, but otherwise it has, so it seems, to be Man or men; and it makes no sense for a feminist to grant judicial authority to her adversary.

As the nineteenth century progressed, "philanthropy" acquired, not without reason, something of a bad name. Professional "philanthropists," the Mrs. Pardiggle and her like, with their "impersonal" goodwill and intolerably meddling ways, became a favorite bugbear and butt for satire in Victorian Britain, whether in the novels of Dickens or the autobiographies of Beatrice Webb. One remembers that wonderfully awful "At Home" given by Octavia Hill to the old tenants of her model dwellings, as described by her fellow social worker Henrietta Barnett. "I recall the guests coming in shyly by the back entrance, and the rather exaggerated cordiality of Miss Octavia's greeting in the effort to make them feel welcome; and Miss Miranda's bright tender way of speaking to everyone exactly alike, were they rich or poor."[4] Lionel Trilling summed up the criticism when he wrote: "Some paradox of our nature leads us, when once we have made our fellow men the objects of our enlightened interest, to go on to make them the objects of our pity, then of our wisdom, ultimately of our coercion."[5]

For Marx, these were not just distortions of philanthropy but its very essence. In *The Poverty of Philosophy*, he has some telling pages on the "philanthropic" school in economics. It is, he writes, "the humanitarian school carried to perfection. It denies the necessity of antagonism; it wants to turn all men into bourgeois.... The philanthropists want to retain the categories which express bourgeois relations, without the antagonism which constitutes them and is inseparable from them. They think they are seriously fighting bourgeois practice, and they are more bourgeois than the others."[6] From this, it follows logically that, for him, the role of the "disinterested" Gladstone-type politician is a mere cloak for "bourgeois" class interest.

Nevertheless, a puzzle remains in our minds. For it is really very hard to see in what sense Marx himself was not a philanthropist. He is, at least, like Engels, a clear – and indeed inspiring – example of someone devoting his life to the interests of a group not his own. (What had the son of a counselor-at-law to the appeal court in Trier, or the son of a wealthy cotton manufacturer, to do with the proletariat, German or otherwise?) Further, are not some of Marx's reasonings about "class" reminiscent of the ones people have such hard words for on the part of "philanthropists"? The "objective" interests that Marx attributes to a "class," regardless of what the members of that class think them to be – vide *The Eighteenth Brumaire* – are they not most simply described as what someone from another class *philanthropically* wants on their behalf? Lenin, later, was frank that "the development of an independent ideology among the workers, as a result of their own struggle," was out of the question; at most all they were capable of was "trade-union consciousness." Thus the work had to be done for them, by "the representatives of the well-to-do, the intellectuals."

There seems in fact to be some bad faith involved in using the term "philanthropy" as a smear word or slur. If Marx and Gladstone and Beatrice Webb are all, in a certain sense, in the same philanthropic boat, no blanket condemnation of politics-on-behalf-of-others – of politics on behalf of a group to which does not belong – can legitimately be made.

This is not to say that there is no need for a critique of philanthropy. Here "humanism" might be said to have something special to offer, in its stress on the question of who is saying what to whom and from where; that is, from what personal standpoint.

To give an example or two: there is, or at least used to be, a kind of "middle class" progressive who, out of a sense of guilt, liked to exaggerate the difficulty of moving from the "working class" to the "middle class," speaking of it as though it were a kind of defection or corruption. Such progressives would, as it were, urge the worker, like Matthew Arnold to the Scholar Gipsy, to "fly our paths, our feverish contact fly," would exhort him to go all out for his own interest and not listen to the canting politicians when they talked about the "national" interest, for all they meant was their *own* interest. The critique that a humanist would make is that this was not the sort of advice such speakers would ever have listened to themselves. It was *contemptuous* advice, tacitly declaring that "the working-class are not like us."

Another neat example arises in connection with the famous late-Victorian settlement known as Toynbee Hall, in London's East End. The scheme was for some fifteen or twenty university-trained young men to live for a year or two in a college-style hall in Whitechapel, perhaps spending their working day in careers elsewhere in the city, but devoting all rest of their

time to classes, lectures, and discussion groups for the benefit of the local poor. It was not expected of them that they
should share the life of the poor, but rather that they should
show the poor the possibility of "a more elevated, a more gracious, more fulfilling life, a life that the poor could not hope
to emulate but that could, by its example, enrich and enlarge
them." Canon Barnett, the founder of the hall, said that the
residents (or "settlers," as he liked to call them, evoking colonial echoes) came to live among the poor "to learn as much
as to teach, to receive as much as to give." Indeed, it was often
affirmed that the institution was primarily for the benefit of
the "settlers" themselves, as a means of developing their "best
self."

There are various things about this to give one alarm or
make one squirm, but the central logical fallacy can be stated
with some exactness. It is again a matter, as one might say, of
not examining the pronouns in a sentence. For it might be
all right for Barnett to think of the residents as an exhibition
of all that was gracious and endearing in educated life, but it
could scarcely be all right – it must be entirely self-defeating –
for them to think this themselves. Whatever a "best self" can
be, it can hardly thrive on a diet of unlimited self-approval.

But the logic of philanthropy is altogether complex, as another example will bring home, once more concerning Wordsworth. The fatal flaw in his "Old Cumberland Beggar" (see
chapter 1) was the tacit suggestion that the old man is suffering
all this pain *on our behalf* – which is something that Wordsworth
is certainly not in a position to say. On the other hand, we may
perhaps guess at the poem he really meant to write by considering a rather similar poem of his – the magnificent sonnet
"To Toussaint L'Ouverture" – in which he is saying something
equally strange but that, this time, he *is* in a position to say.

The poem is again, in a sense, an extraordinarily "callous"
one. Wordsworth is writing while Toussaint is still in prison,
and he rubs it in that Toussaint will find no comfort this side
of the grave. Nevertheless, he exhorts him to "live and take

comfort," since he has "left behind powers" that will work for him; he is going to be of value to *us,* as an object for our imagination and to remind us of "exultations, agonies, / And love, and man's unconquerable mind." Toussaint the man is swept aside with a grand, untender decisiveness, and it is made clear that the idea of suffering it all on *our* behalf is no more than a ruthless poetic fiction.

It brings home to us the unique place Wordsworth occupies in the history of philanthropy: his frankness in disregarding the feelings of the individual in favor of those of humanity at large, but also, and more strikingly, in asserting that pleasure is an indispensable element in benevolence. We cannot do good to others, so he argues, unless we are happy ourselves, and shall only influence for evil if we try. Hence, it is a moral duty to make oneself happy; and it a moral duty for him to retire from the scenes of his failed political hopes and search out true sources of happiness among the mountains of Cumberland. When he and Dorothy retire to the Lakes, it is thus with the explicit intention of being an engine for good in the new philanthropic way. Nor can it be said that the hope was illusory: he did become an engine for good, and it *was* in a new way: he became the Lourdes to which many an angst-ridden Victorian intellectual resorted. Nevertheless, the more one reads Wordsworth, the more struck one is by the strange harshness of his philanthropy. It is summed up in his Wanderer in *The Excursion* – a figure who, as he admits, represents himself. The Wanderer, according to Wordsworth, is peculiarly fitted to enter into the sorrows of others because he has had no sorrows himself. This is a very odd theory, but there is no doubt that it is what Wordsworth says. The Wanderer, or Pedlar, has cultivated his affections in the fields, all alone, "In solitude and solitary thought,"

> . . . in his steady course,
> No piteous revolutions he had felt,
> No wild varieties of joy and grief.

Being therefore unpreoccupied by his own sorrows, his "heart lay open" and turned to sympathy toward mankind: ". . . He could *afford* to suffer / With those whom he saw suffer."

But let us return to politics and to the distinction made at the beginning of this chapter: that is to say, between politics on behalf of a group one belongs to and politics on behalf of one to which one does not. It will be seen that it does not exhaust the possibilities, for neither description fits "politics of the person."

By convention, the birth of "politics of the person" is dated from the Paris "events" of 1968. The "events" constituted a violent reaction against Stalinism and a decision that the way forward lay neither with Stalinism nor with democracy and the fallacies of "representation." In a conversation with Michel Foucault a year or two after the "events" of May 1968, Gilles Deleuze told him: "You were the first to teach us something absolutely fundamental: the indignity of speaking for others. We ridiculed representation and said it was finished, but we failed to draw the consequences of this 'theoretical' conversion – to appreciate the theoretical fact that only those directly concerned can speak in a practical way on their own behalf."[7] By the rejection of "representation" is meant a repudiation of democracy and representative government (though also of the idea of literature as representation, rather than as "production"), and what this implies, it should be observed, is a politics entirely free from philanthropy. In a certain sense, for all Marx's railings against philanthropists, it is hard to deny that Marxism was a philanthropy. Thus "politics of the person," with its insistence that everyone should speak with their own distinctive voice, unmediated by "representation" or action "on behalf of" others, realizes what Marx merely dreamed of. I have tried to indicate some of the traps that lie in wait for philanthropy, and from these at least "politics of the person" is quite free.

The advent of "politics of the person" coincided with the

sudden rise to worldwide fame of Jacques Lacan. In an article about Lacan in the *London Review of Books* (6 December 1990), Sherry Turkle writes:

May–June 1968 was an explosion of speech and desire. It called for the invention of new political forms that looked not to the politics of traditional political parties but to a politics of the person. For a short while the "events" looked like a revolution in the making, but then suddenly they were over. After the events, people were left hungry for a way to continue to think about sexuality and self-expression as part of a revolutionary movement; for a way to think about the personal as the political and social. "Thinking through the events" required a theory which integrated society and individual. Lacan provided that theory.

For several years after 1968, according to Turkle, French social and political thought was dominated by Lacanism, "in particular the notions that people are constituted by language, that our discourse embodies the society beyond, and that there is no autonomous ego."

"Politics of the person" was thus a movement away from humanitarian politics and economism, and toward – in the words of a manifesto in *Tel Quel* in the summer of 1968 – "a radical subverting of the individual's secure self-identification in language, his or her *subjectivity* understood as the manner in which individuals recognise themselves as subjects in and of any linguistic text." It was a form of politics that did not need to involve collective action; and it went along with "textual politics" and the hegemony of Theory in general. *Tel Quel* called for "the construction of a theory which works towards the critical integration of the most developed practices of philosophy, linguistics, semiology, psychoanalysis, 'literature', and the history of science." Any ideological undertaking that did not "present itself in an advanced theoretical form" and settled instead for "bringing together, under eclectic or sentimental headings, individuals and under-politicised activities," was to be regarded as counterrevolutionary, "inasmuch as it fails to recognise the process of the class-struggle."[8] It is the moment of birth of "cultural studies"; that is, the theory that literature, and discussion of literature, have no properties of their own and cannot be kept separate from all other forms of discourse, and that political ends can be fought for, and a blow struck against "the ideology of perpetual domination," by challenging (as J. Fekete has called it) "the fetish of achieved form" in works of literature.[9]

Another name for the legacy of 1968 would thus be "postmodernism." Nevertheless, it will be best to cling to the phrase "politics of the person," or, as it is also sometimes called, "the politics of difference"; and since the larger part of the political theory and writing that is around today – radical-feminist politics, gay and lesbian politics, black politics, and so on – belongs to this "politics of difference," it is important to be clear about its structure. One way of doing this is by thinking of the British Labour movement in the late nineteenth and early twentieth centuries. This was, very evidently, not a politics of "difference." The claim of its leaders was that the underprivileged and exploited were, humanly speaking, not only as good as their masters and exploiters but no different from them. If at present there was a gulf between them and the educated classes, this was because an evil social system prevented them from realizing their full potential: it had nothing to do with any desire to be, or think themselves, different. Of course, among their socially privileged supporters, there were a few sentimentalists who, masochistically, liked to believe the workers were "better" – nobler, less corrupted – but this was a side issue. What the leaders of the movement appealed to, explicitly, was an idea of general humanity and the unity of the human species. According to postmodernist theory, they fell into the trap of "essentialism."

Marx has an acute comment in *German Ideology* that helps throw light on what the British Labour movement was doing:

Each new class which puts itself in the place of one ruling before it, is compelled, merely, in order to carry through its aim, to represent its

66

*interest as the common interest of all the members of society, put in an
ideal form; it will give its ideas the form of universality, and represent
them as the only rational, universally valid ones. The class making a
revolution appears from the very start, merely because it is opposed to a
class, not as a class but as the representative of the whole of society; it
appears as the whole mass of society confronting the one ruling class.*[10]

The contrast, when we come to "politics of the person," or
"the politics of difference," is really very great. It constitutes
the third possibility, the third interpretation of "behalf," that
I mentioned earlier. It is not "politics on behalf of a group
that one does not belong to" (in other words, strictly "philanthropic" politics); and, if it is "politics on behalf of a group
that one belongs to oneself," it is so in a way very much unlike
the model of the old British Labour movement or the "class"
model offered by Marx.

For an important thing about it, catching the eye at once,
is that it is a politics without (unconcerned with) a polis. By its
definition, a practitioner of "the politics of difference" is not
in the business of presenting himself or herself, or his or her
associates, as "the representative of the whole of society." It
is not even part of the program to say what society should be
like, except that it should respect "difference."

In anything save an anarchist utopia, the demand for respect for one's difference has of course to be addressed, first
of all, to the state. This raises the question, what kind of state?
Asked what sort of society he or she would favor, a practitioner of "politics of the person" might very possibly answer
"pluralism." But, as this book has insisted rather repetitiously,
"pluralism," an intensely desirable disposition on the part of
an individual, is really not a political concept; it offers no
political content not already contained in "democracy." As a
political doctrine, "pluralism" is purely utopian; that is to say,
it is unpolitical. It is a millennial yearning, such as the one expressed by Roland Barthes: "Utopia (*à la* Fourier): . . . a world
in which there would no longer be anything but differences,

so that to be differentiated would no longer mean to be excluded."[11]

The May "events" saw a rethinking of the idea of "revolution." Alan Sheridan, in his *Michel Foucault*, writes that those who clung to the idea of revolution as the seizure of state power by "the people" were prisoners of an outmoded rhetoric. What *was* truly revolutionary, says Sheridan, was the idea that "the state was everywhere and therefore the 'revolution' had to be everywhere, ubiquitous as well as permanent." By this definition, "politics of the person" becomes a form of power politics, dedicated to combating power – power not in its centralized manifestations, but in its disseminated and "capillary" form.

The success of the May events, according to Sheridan, was "the discovery by small groups of people of an unsuspected creativity, the capacity for inventing new forms of social relations, a desire and an ability to run their own affairs."[12] They are generous words, and probably have some truth in them. The commune, as a "new form of social relations," has not always been a failure. This would be the nonpolitical fruit of the "events."

On the other hand, so far as the word "politics" is concerned, it seems that "the politics of difference" must be called "politics on behalf of oneself" (the word "behalf" therefore becoming not much more than a *façon de parler*). The structure of "politics of the person" can be seen to take the form of "How can my own personal situation be put to use as a power base?"

In *Culture and Imperialism*, Edward Said makes it a damning criticism of imperialism that it caused people to think of themselves merely as *one* thing – whereas, as he says, labels like "Indian" or "woman" or "American" ought to be no more than "starting-points." "Imperialism consolidated the mixture of cultures and identities on a global scale. But its worst and most paradoxical gift was to allow people to believe that they were only, mainly, exclusively, white, or black, or Western, or oriental."[13] Now, whether or not this is true of imperialism, it exactly describes the system of "politics of the person." "Politics of the person" aims precisely at intensifying one's own sense of being *one* thing (a woman, or gay, or black, and so forth), making systematic use of "consciousness-raising" to this end. The wish to be in oneself the whole of humanity, the desire to project oneself into alien experience, must come from a very different part of the mind from the wish to affirm one's "difference." Indeed, it hardly seems as if they could be reconciled.

"Politics of the person," in its guise as the "politics of difference," poses writers with a problem regarding their audience. The critic Alan Sinfield, having to review Thom Gunn's *The Man With Night Sweats,* a volume of poems dealing with the poet's "gay" life and friends, under the shadow of the AIDS pandemic, wrote to Gunn, in *Gay Times* and elsewhere, asking him whether he regarded himself as a "gay poet" or merely "a poet who is gay." He had, he says, two thoughts in mind. "One is whether the traditional idea of poetry – associated with the Faber slim volume – has not run its course as an effective cultural form ['it's doubtful how far that general, "human" voice of traditional poetry can be trusted any more']. The other is whether a more valuable project, anyway, is not to reinforce a beleaguered gay subculture (similar considerations would apply to other subordinated groups). The arguments are connected, for the customary idea of writing and reading poetry assumes an essential humanity that ineluctably effaces subcultural difference."[14] Gunn's answer was that sometimes he thought of himself as writing for a gay audience, but usually he didn't think very precisely about the matter at all; in the main, he felt he was using a voice that was not universal or "human," and not specifically gay either, but simply his own. "When I write about my life as a gay man, or with a gay emphasis, I am implicitly saying that I don't have to put on a special voice to speak about such matters." But here Gunn actually understates what he has done. In *The Man With Night Sweats* he goes out of his way, by formality of diction and versification that is obtrusively traditional, also a more or less explicit allusion to Jonsonian "civility," to exploit the resonances of "canonical" English literature. It is exactly his way of making the point that, to use Sinfield's words, "in the face of Aids, gay community is more, not less, necessary and rewarding." It is a beautifully conceived enterprise, cunningly making appeal, precisely, to the "general 'human' voice of traditional poetry."

It is of course a charge often made against "canonical" English literature that it acts as a monolithic tyranny, obliterating subcultural difference. Alan Sinfield quotes Seamus Heaney, who describes, feelingly, the painful dilemma of writers on the margins of English culture. However, Heaney sees it as without issue. The writers long to escape the "established discourse" but are condemned by their "auditory imagination" to stay within it: "Whether they are feminists in reaction against the patriarchy of language or nativists in full cry with the local accents of their vernacular, whether they write Anglo-Irish or Afro-English or Lallans, all writers of what has been called 'nation language' are caught on the forked stick of their love of the English language itself. Helplessly, they kiss the rod of the consciousness which subjugated them."

It is possible, though, to look at the problem from a different angle. For a subculture is something rare, unique, and sui generis, and "the politics of difference" – from both components of the phrase – would not really be adapted to nurture it. As regards "politics," this would be because politics is not concerned with phenomena-as-they-are (their intrinsic quality), but with the use to which they can be put. (Experience shows that to politicize a subculture is often the quickest way to kill it.) And as regards "difference," it is because, if we take the term in a Structuralist sense, it implies that no cultural phenomenon is meaningful in itself; it has meaning only in terms of other things and as part of a signifying system. By proclaiming and cherishing its "difference," in the "politics of difference" sense, a subculture is affirming its indissoluble bondage to establishment culture, as that culture's "other."

It is not in politics or in the concept of "difference" that we shall find respect for the rare, the autonomous, and the irreplaceable. The place for this if anywhere, it strikes one, is aesthetics. One thinks of Gerard Manley Hopkins and his love of "all things counter, original, spare, strange." There is a beautiful and suggestive remark in a letter of his to Robert Bridges. He is discussing his poem "Henry Purcell" and the line "Have an eye to the sakes of him, quaint moonmarks, to his pelted plumage," and he tells Bridges: "*Sake* is a word I find it convenient to use. It is the *sake* of 'for the sake of,' *forsake, namesake, keepsake.* I mean by it the being a thing has outside itself, as a voice by its echo, a face by its reflection, a body by its shadow, a man by his name, fame, or memory, *and also* that in the thing by virtue of which especially it has this being abroad, and that is something distinctive, marked, specifically or individually speaking."[15]

The phrase "for the sake of" has affinities with the phrase "on behalf of." Hopkins's notion of a "sake" as a real entity helps one to imagine a version of philanthropy, or action "for the *sake* of" others, in which there would never be danger of infringing those others' independence.

6

The Politics of Gender

W here the question of audience – that is so say, whom one is writing for – is a particularly burning one is, of course, feminist writing. It would scarcely have occurred to anyone that, in *Le Deuxième sexe,* Simone de Beauvoir was not addressing men just as much as she was addressing women. This was plainly essential to the purpose of book, the last words of which urge that "by and through their natural differentiation men and women [should] unequivocally affirm their brotherhood." By contrast, much of current feminist writing (and not only of a "postmodernist" kind) is fairly clearly addressed to all-women readerships. The implications of this are far-reaching; indeed, they are actually not too easy to get one's mind round.

Le Deuxième sexe may fairly be called an example of "modernist," as opposed to "postmodernist," feminism, and its drift is that ideas of femininity are purely relational: they are no more than the complement or "verso" of ideas of masculinity, just as ideas of masculinity are the complement of ideas of femininity – the whole construction being, as one might say, a human *folie à deux.* From which it follows that, in the very nature of things, it would be absurd to imagine this construction being modified unilaterally – by women alone, or by men alone. Feminist writing of this school is bound in logic to address itself to a mixed-sex readership.

Now what is wrong with *Le Deuxième sexe,* in my view, is its talk of "natural differentiation" between the sexes and of "brotherhood" and "equality" between them. The true implication of de Beauvoir's book, it seems to me, is something more simple and absolute: it is that, as human beings, men

73

and women are not "equals" but, rather, exactly the same – that gender, as opposed to sex, is *entirely* a cultural construction. This principle is a precious one, and any weakening over it seems to bring a fatal train of confusions, paradoxes, and vicious circles.

It is not, after all, as if there is anything especially strange or even unfamiliar about this account of "gender." Lévi-Strauss writes: "Passage from the state of Nature to the state of Culture is marked by man's ability to view biological relations as a series of contrasts; . . . duality, alternation, opposition, and symmetry, whether under definite or vague forms, constitute not so much phenomena to be explained as fundamental and immediately given data of social reality."[1] This is a powerful insight, and it offers an obvious explanation of the concept of gender. If culture requires binary oppositions as a way of thinking about "social reality," what more inevitable than that it should seize on the male-female contrast – in the same spirit as on the contrast between the "raw" and the "cooked"?

Assuming this to be true, then the next step is easily imagined. A woman, having been "essentialized" as such – that is to say, credited with special and intrinsic qualities constituting her kind as a human "variety," or subspecies – will internalize this operation and willingly (though unconsciously) embrace the idea of possessing an "otherness." This has the character of retaliation and would be best described as a political move, a first step into inauthenticity. The fact that physical difference (difference-within-a-likeness) is erotically attractive to heterosexuals would of course be a temptation, on both sides, to imagine it reflected a human difference. The imagined difference will be *relational,* in the sense defined by Simone de Beauvoir, the supposed "feminine" qualities being the verso of "masculine" ones.

The result, in the more developed stages of social existence, has, as we know, been horribly stifling and oppressive to women. Thus, to dismantle and unthink the superstition of "gender," or at all events its cruel, oppressive, and stultifying aspects, to lay the ghost of female "otherness," is a most important duty – moreover obviously not an impossible one. A fair amount has been done in that direction already. The task is to recognize the fact that "gender" and female "otherness" are an illusion – that humanly speaking men and women are exactly the same, and each man or woman contains the whole potential of the human species. But from this it follows logically that the unthinking of gender can only be done by men and women jointly.

Of these three concepts, gender, class, and race, gender is by far the most deeply rooted, and it is doubtful whether it could ever be finally dissolved. Nor indeed would it make sense to want this or aspire to do more than purge it of its harmful elements.

However, the function, as symbolic language, of dichotomies like masculine/feminine evidently belongs to an exceedingly remote stage of communal life – that of an original passage from nature to culture; and the thought strikes one that they may be out of place anywhere save at this "primitive" social stage. It may be right to look with suspicion on later imitations.

I am thinking, for instance, of "color." It does not appear that a color-problem existed in the ancient world. Was Saint Augustine black? Nobody seems to have taken any interest in the matter in his day. The "black"/"white" dichotomy seems to be rooted in a specific historical circumstance, the seventeenth-century slave trade. It must, however, have been selected as a signifier for largely the same reasons as sex; that is to say, its simplicity – a human being with a "black" skin exhibiting the same kind of eye-catching resemblance-with-a-difference to one with a "white" skin as a woman does to a man. Upon a neat dichotomy of this kind, an enormous structure of cultural and political meaning can be reared, and all sorts of fantastic rationalizations imposed. There can even come to be talk of a black *race* and a white *race*, though anthro-

pologically speaking no idea could be more absurd. To unthink "color" looks like an important task.

One may also think of gayness, in this connection. It looks
as if gayness might be a belated extension of the ancient "gender" dichotomization. At a certain moment in history (a fairly
late one, according to Foucault), a man or woman erotically
attracted to his or her own sex comes to be told that this is
part of his or her human *identity* (just as gender had already
been fixed on humans as their *identity*). From this, the inference is drawn, by homosexuals as well as by their heterosexual
enemies or sympathizers, that a homosexual man must really
in some sense be a woman, and a homosexual woman must in
some sense really be a man. For proof of the grip of this way
of thinking, we need look no further than Proust's *Sodome et
Gomorrhe;* and, to the extent that it still operates, it would of
course be a prime candidate for "unthinking."

Such a picture of things as I have been drawing seems to
me, actually, very plausible. But at all events it would seem
one has either firmly to adopt some such theory or firmly reject it; it is not an issue on which one can equivocate, or have
one's cake and eat it. The theory that female "otherness" is an
illusion and the theory that women *as such* possess "intrinsic"
qualities are diametrically opposed; and if the former is correct, it must follow that the latter (which you might call the
"essentialist" theory) is a dangerous and destructive illusion,
from which one should be making every effort to awake. It
will cause endless confusion, and be a dangerous form of bad
faith, to talk at one moment as if gender (or color or gayness)
were purely cultural or political constructs, and the next moment as if they were written into the makeup of humans at
birth. It is here that the trouble lies with a good deal of radical feminist writing.

To take an example, there is hardly a single contributor to
the Linda Nicholson symposium *Feminism/Postmodernism* who
does not equivocate on this issue. Even Christine di Stefano,
in a very honest and lucid study of what she calls the "Dilem-

mas of Difference," offers a having-it-both-ways statement on the matter. She writes:

The concept of gender has made it possible for feminists to simultaneously explain and delegitimize the presumed homology between biological and social sex differences. At the same time, however, gender (rather than sex) differences have emerged as highly significant, salient features which do more to divide and distinguish men and women from each other than to make them parts of some larger, complementary, humanistic whole. In other words, the feminist analysis of gender has undone one version of presumably basic difference, thought to be rooted in nature, and come up with another, albeit more debatably basic than the previous one.[2]

Try as one will, one cannot read these sentences otherwise than as saying: feminists have shown the physical difference of the sexes both *not to be* and to *be* socially significant; they have proved that it both *does not* and *does* bestow different basic identities on men and for women. She has been led, so far as one can see, into a pure self-contradiction, and the reason why is characteristic of radical feminist writing. It is that she has been opportunistic: she has posed the problem of the nature of gender as a political one from the very start – as if indistinguishable from the question, What theory of gender will bring women the best political returns? Indeed, a page or two later she states this openly. "In asking how basic gender differences *are*, we are also asking how basic *we want them to be* for particular purposes and ends. This is really what the feminist debate about gender these days is all about. It could not be otherwise, since gender itself is a product of and a contribution to modernist discourse; it is about conventional forms of meaning, practice, and representation and not at all about foundations, whether natural or metaphysical."[3]

Every contributor to Nicholson's *Feminism/Postmodernism* is, of course, up against the same baffling problem: that, powerful though its insights are, postmodernism is no encouragement whatever to concerted political action – not, anyway, in the traditional sense of "political." As di Stefano puts it, feminist politics is bound up with a particular "constituency" – that is, women; and postmodernism is bound to want to dissolve this universalizing concept "women," regarding the fiction of "woman" as oppressive and running roughshod over multiple differences among and between women.

Susan Bordo, in "Feminism, Postmodernism and Gender-Scepticism," argues for pragmatism. It is, she contends, simply too soon for feminists to adopt postmodernist theory. "Most of our institutions have barely begun to absorb the message of modernist social criticism; surely, it is too soon to let them off the hook via postmodern heterogeneity and instability." A postmodern "view from everywhere" could, she says, be as false an illusion of detachment as the traditionalist "view from nowhere," and skepticism about "gender" could actually, unknowingly, be leading women back into captivity: it could be helping to reproduce "white, male knowledge/power." However, by a fatality characteristic of these arguments, what is left of Bordo's feminist program, when it has cut its links with postmodernism, is almost comically crude and Tammany Hall. It is for women to go on acquiring power over "grant, program, and conference guidelines and descriptions," and "hiring, tenure, promotion, publications etc."

By contrast, Donna Haraway, in "A Manifesto for Cyborgs," goes the whole way with postmodernism and ends up in another of the dilemmas it holds in store – a dilemma of the type one might call "recursive" – that is to say, resulting from something fatally self-reflexive in the theory itself. Her essay (it was written back in 1985, at the height of the "cybernetics" revolution) is a cunning and pyrotechnic fantasy about how women might escape "phallocracy" by allying themselves with machines and animals: how they might create for themselves a "dispersed" or "monstrous" identity, a "disassembled and reassembled collective and personal self," thereby learning how not to be Man, the embodiment of Western logos. At a certain point, however, she runs up against the problem of

78

her own authority in speaking. The objection to Socialism and Marxism, she says, is their "unintended erasure of polyvocal, unassimilable, radical difference made visible in anticolonial discourse and practice." Their trouble is that they are forms of totalization; they are not willing to offer themselves as a merely "partial" explanation. But then, she says, the same is true of radical feminism, and the same is true of her own theories. Any system of thought whatever is bound to be unfair to "polyvocality."

In their different tones, pragmatic, apocalyptic, or other, all these writers agree that the question of gender is plagued with dilemmas. In her "Dilemmas of Difference," Christine di Stefano sets them out soberly and pessimistically. There are, she writes, three "strategic forms" for posing the relationship between contemporary Western feminism and old-style "enlightened" humanistic rationalism. They are (1) feminist rationalism; (2) feminist antirationalism; (3) feminist postrationalism.

The rationalist position, according to her, declares that a common respect is due to all people because they are rational, and women have been unfairly treated in this respect through an insidious assumption that they are less rational, and by corollary more "natural," than men. Rationalism demands that "difference" be repudiated, both in theory and practice, so that women can take their rightful place in society as the "nondifferentiated equals of men."

By contrast, antirationalism, she says, attempts to revalorize the feminine "nature" denigrated by rationalist culture – a culture that "opposes itself to nature, the body, natural contingency and intuition." Antirationalism offers a vision of a social order designed to accommodate women in their feminized difference, rather than as "imperfect copies of the Everyman."

Postrationalism, on the other hand, wants to transcend the discourse of rationalism. It wishes to counterpoise a proliferation of differences against the single difference of gender and to expose dualistic "difference" as a weapon of the very system of domination to which it is ostensibly opposed.

The postrationalist position, says di Stefano, is both appealing and unnerving. It suggests that *a* feminist standpoint, like *the* feminist movement, would be an oppressive and totalizing fiction, just as humanism has been, and that women ought to content themselves with fractured identities. They should adopt as a political position what Sandra Harding, in an essay in the same volume, calls "permanent partiality." But, asks di Stefano, could that not, from another point of view, just be seen as sour grapes? And would not postmodernism, if seriously adopted by feminists, make a feminist politics impossible? Is the risk of a linkage with postmodernism worth taking? The language of postmodernism, says di Stefano, has reappropriated the vocabulary of "pluralism"; and pluralism (à la Richard Rorty), which pictures Theory as a huge "conversation" among a variety of fractured participants, is not a recognition of difference but a reduction to *in*difference. "It is," she writes, "as if postmodernism has returned us to the falsely innocent indifference of the very humanism to which it stands opposed: a rerun, in updated garb, of the modernist case of the incredible shrinking women."

Her brief and half-dispirited answer to these dilemmas is that, so far, there *is* no answer. The dilemmas have to be lived with, and they suggest that "gender is basic in ways that we have yet fully to understand," that it functions as "a difference that makes a difference."

It is here that one wants to say she may have ignored a clue, in the form of the question, Whom is she writing for? Is she addressing everyone, or only women? The question, through being censored out, makes itself felt all the more strongly. Let us consider a theory that belongs in her "antirationalist" category, I mean the argument, put forward by Carol McMillan and others, that "women's work" should be revalorized: that the everyday life practices of women, particularly child rearing, call for reevaluation as complex, thoughtful, and (in an important sense) *rational* activities.

The question that this evidently prompts is, "revalorized in whose eyes?" They can hardly be the eyes of God, nor of some imagined government (for only a benevolent despot is likely to undergo such a change of heart). Yet if what is meant is, *women's* eyes, the outlook amounts to a very extreme antifeminism, implying that women should give up wanting to be business executives or prime ministers or professors. So the only alternative left, it would seem, is that women's work should be revalorized in *men's* eyes – which is an appeal to men, the "other," that no self-respecting feminist could possibly make. There seems no escape from this dilemma, so long as men are credited with "otherness" (and thus as being, by definition, no fit audience for feminist writing).

Of course, there are men who, in philanthropic fashion, make offers of help to feminists, but this tactic gives one a disagreeable feeling. Richard Rorty, in an article on "Feminism and Pragmatism" in *Radical Philosophy*,[4] claims that Pragmatists like himself can make sense of radical feminism in a way that Kantian "universalists" and "realists" are not equipped to. "Universalists" assume that all the "logical space" required for moral deliberation is already available, and "realists" assume that there is an unchanging morality "out there" to be tracked down by Reason. Feminists, on the other hand, need to invent a new reality, and also a new vocabulary in which to describe it; and till they have done so, their demands are doomed to sound – anyway, to universalists and realists – as merely visionary and crazy. He thinks it is a pity feminists sometimes attempt *not* to sound crazy and resort to "realist" rhetoric; though no doubt, he says, a certain amount of hypocrisy is scarcely to be avoided, and "practical politics will doubtless often require feminists to speak with the universalist vulgar." He thinks feminists ought to band together in exclusive clubs, where they can achieve "semantic authority" over themselves, as a prelude to achieving it over others. – But how, one asks oneself, is it compatible with Pragmatism, the friend of polyvocality, to credit any language with "authority"? One seems to be hearing the sort of rather insulting advice that the privileged used to give to the working man, advice of a kind they would resent if anyone offered it to themselves.

And who are these Pragmatists? "We" (the Pragmatists), says Rorty, are "just trying to help women out of the traps men have constructed for them." That "we" seems to call for some unpacking, like the "we liberals" in whose name Rorty also likes sometimes to speak. Where does this body exist? How does it come to be exempt from the gender war? If feminists take it up on its promise of help, will it not be liable to melt away, leaving a solitary man, speaking on behalf of Pragmatism, not of Pragmatists? The hint that Rorty has troops to throw in is simply a touch of political fantasy.

Radical feminism is the most advanced example of "politics of the person," and its complications paralyse the mind. It is my impression that the feminist problem with gender, with all its paradoxes and vicious circles, is an exitless maze, and the only escape is by the door by which one came in. That is to say, one must retract the fatal first step: that of supposing that, as human beings, women are different from men.

7

Humanisms

It would seem as if in adopting the standpoint I have been proposing – and, as it were, taking it on myself to stand up for the human *species* – I might want to call myself a "humanist," and I would gladly do so if I could be clear what it would mean. But the paradox is, it is from anti-"humanists," such as Heidegger, Lévi-Strauss, Barthes, and Foucault that one gets the best idea of "humanism" as a creed to be reckoned with. The implications of anti-"humanism" are profound and far-reaching; but they also, when one thinks them through, can appear extravagant and fantastic and contrary to reason and experience. It is anti-"humanism," if anything, that will make one want to call oneself a "humanist."

Which instantly brings into question that word "creed." To describe oneself as a "humanist" has traditionally implied something about revealed religion: it has been a way of arguing that human beings must get on without religion (by which is generally meant Christianity), and moreover that they are perfectly able to do so and can construct a satisfactory ethics from their own secular and "human" resources. This would be the primary sense of the word. Beyond this, the implications are less clear. Not all humanists would call themselves atheists (some might prefer to use the word "agnostic"), nor would every humanist claim to be a "rationalist"; and there would be even less agreement on other large topics of the day, like science, or sex, or multiculturalism, or the idea of a world-state.

Humanism has, moreover, often been accused of being parasitic on the religion that it has rejected, and really with a good deal of justice: for, for one thing, it has shown a dangerous fondness for words borrowed from the religious vocabulary, like "faith" and "redemption," "crusade" and "sacrifice." Indeed, one can go one step further. In reading humanist writings, it is hard not to feel that much of the pleasure of being a humanist lies in *enjoying* one's freedom from religion, or at least drawing a powerful emotional drive from it (for instance, from the exciting idea of having been "abandoned" by God). Thus humanism, if it is not to wilt and perish, has to keep religion constantly in mind. In this sense, too, it is parasitic and not really equipped to stand on its own.

It is hard to see any escape from these criticisms. Nevertheless, in this chapter, I will sketch one or two of the better-known "humanist" movements of the century.

F. C. S. SCHILLER

There was, for instance, the movement launched by the Oxford philosopher F. C. S. Schiller in his *Humanism* in 1903. His book was designed as an antidote to neo-Hegelianism of the F. H. Bradley stamp and proposed to begin philosophy not from the "presuppositionless" basis beloved of a priori philosophers but from the everyday world of human experience. Schiller's "humanism" was, in fact, merely the name he gave to one aspect of William James's Pragmatism; that is, the theory that truths are man-made rather than entities independent of man and existent from all eternity. It did not have anything special to say about "man," merely proposing, in the spirit of Plato's Protagoras, to make him the point of reference for all philosophical inquiry.

IRVING BABBITT

More in the usual style of humanisms (i.e., with their kinship to religion) was the "New Humanism" of Irving Babbitt and Paul Elmer More, much in the news for a year or two during the late 1920s. Babbitt's doctrine was an entirely eclectic faith, bred out of book-culture – a matter of "siding" with Christianity or Buddhism over this or that issue, or "avoiding the Stoical error," and so on, and it is now best remembered because of T. S. Eliot's essay "The Humanism of Irving Babbitt." Eliot claimed once to have been a disciple of Babbitt, and he affirmed, teasingly, the deepest respect for Babbitt's knowledge of religions, so "infinitely" beyond his own. Nevertheless, he wrote Babbitt's humanism off (very fairly, one is inclined to say) as a shadow of religion, "a product – a by-product – of Protestant theology in its last agonies." Humanism, he said, was "merely the state of mind of a few persons in a few places at a few times" and was conditional on the existence of organized religion: "To exist at all, it is dependent upon some other attitude, for it is essentially critical – I would even say parasitical. It has been, and can still be, of great value; but it will never provide showers of partridges or abundance of manna for the chosen people."[1]

ROMAIN ROLLAND, MERLEAU-PONTY, AND "SOCIALIST HUMANISM"

The "humanism" that, in the person of the "Autodidact," gets such a flaying in Sartre's *La Nausée* (see chapter 3) was essentially a form of Communist fellow-traveling and is represented most vividly and completely in Romain Rolland. Rolland's vast roman-fleuve *L'Annonciatrice* (1933) charts, in the person of its hero, a development from aesthetic humanism toward political commitment or engagement; and its final volume (in the words of his biographer) "turns on the coming to communism of the enchanted soul, that is, the Western humanist intellectual."[2] When in 1930 Rolland was attacked in a Soviet literary review for being an "individualist" and a "humanist," he replied indignantly that he was one of the most loyal friends and defenders of the Soviet Union, and he was bringing humanism over to its side. "I bring to you, I bring into your camp, the camp of the workers who are masters of their destiny, the sacred banners of freedom of thought and humanity. Do not reject them! Be proud of them! Rejoice that they come to fight on your side. . . . The gods of the old world, *freedom, humanity,* are deserting the camp of your enemies. They are coming over to you. Welcome them! And grasp the hand of him who leads them to you. They shake your hand – fraternally."[3]

It is a curious fact that, not only did Rolland coin the term "engagement," it was he who gave Freud the phrase "the oceanic feeling." The mainspring of his own socialist humanism was, evidently, an "oceanic" feeling of solidarity with mankind and with the workers; and it may be supposed that, in the restaurant scene in Sartre's *La Nausée,* what upsets Roquentin more than anything is the Autodidact's Romain Rollandism.

It was at much the same period that Jacques Maritain attempted to reconcile communist or fellow-traveling "humanism," in the shape of the "heroic" humanism he found in the novels of André Malraux, with the teaching of Aquinas. For a year or two, Maritain's *Humanisme intégral* (1936), pretty much forgotten now, had quite a vogue. This "heroic" or Socialist version of humanism, moreover, survived the war and found its last notable manifestation in Merleau-Ponty's *Humanisme et terreur: Essai sur le problème communiste* (1947) – a defense of Stalinism on the grounds that only the proletariat could solve the existential conflict of warring "subjectivities." This was so, Merleau-Ponty argued, because the condition of the proletarian was a "universal" one. He was "cut off from all particularity, not by thought and a process of abstraction, but in reality, and through the very substance of his life." If Marxism privileged the workers, it was not as a totality of individuals but as a particular "condition," to be regarded as human above all others. It was because, "through the inherent logic of their condition, through their most instinctive ways of life, regardless of all messianic illusion, the proletarians 'who are not gods' are, and are alone, in a position to realise humanity."[4] This philosophical mysticism about the proletariat became a prime target for satire for Raymond Aron in his *Opium of the Intellectuals* (1955).

SARTRE

When, late in 1945, Sartre, the scourge of "humanism," announced to a vast and excited audience that existentialism was a "humanism," it seemed a most extraordinary volte-face. Some of his followers, as Michel Tournier relates, were greatly dismayed and gathered later at a café to mourn their loss, lamenting that their master "had gone and fished up that worn-out old duffer Humanism, still stinking with sweat and 'inner life,' from the trash heap where we had left him." They prophesied gloomily that he would become a Great Man and the Gandhi of Gaullist France. It was a reaction, writes Tournier, that should be taken for what it was – "a liquidation of the father by overgrown adolescents afflicted with the awareness that they owed him everything." Nevertheless, he says, Sartre's dilemma was a real one: that of a Marxist secretly hankering to become a saint.[5]

The purpose of Sartre's talk was to offer a popular defence of existentialism against various reproaches leveled against it by Christians, Marxists, and others. What these complaints came down to was that existentialism was a doctrine of negativity; and – this was the force of the label "a humanism" – Sartre was declaring it to be, on the contrary, a philosophy of optimism and an assertion of human dignity. Also, despite its sulphurous reputation, it was "of all teachings the least scandalous and the most austere."

Having made such ruthless fun of humanism, in its love-for-all-humanity sense, he is at pains to explain that the word can have two different meanings. One meaning holds up man as the end-in-itself and the supreme value. He takes as an example Cocteau's story *Round the World in 80 Hours,* in which a character exclaims, because he is flying over mountains in an aeroplane, that "Man is magnificent!" This, says Sartre, is ridiculous; "for only the dog or the horse would be in a position to pronounce a general judgement upon man and declare that he is magnificent, which they have never been such fools as to do – at least, not as far as I know."[6] Along this road lie the absurdities of Comte's "religion of humanity." There is, however, Sartre argues, another sense of the word, of which the fundamental meaning is that man is *self-surpassing.* "This is humanism, because we remind man that there is no legislator but himself; that he himself, thus abandoned, must decide for himself."

The existentialist, holding that existence comes before essence, denies the existence of a "human nature," given from all eternity and found in every human being. On the contrary, man is nothing else but what he makes of himself. He is not to represent himself as the victim of forces beyond his control – as, for instance, the force of a "grand passion." (Man is as much responsible for his passion as for anything else.) Existentialism places the entire responsibility squarely upon the human being's own shoulders: "And when we say that man is responsible for himself, we do not mean that he is responsible only for his own individuality, but that he is responsible for all men. . . . [I]n choosing for himself he chooses for all humans. For in effect, of all the actions a man may take in order to create himself as he wills to be, there is not one which is not creative, at the same time, of an image of man such as he believes he ought to be."

Everything happens to every man as though the whole human race had its eyes fixed on him, and for this reason he is bound to be burdened with angst. (Those who show no such anxiety are merely disguising their anguish or are in flight from it.) Furthermore, though there is nothing properly to be called "human nature," there is a human universality of *condition*. Man's historical situations are variable: he may be born a slave in a pagan society, or a feudal baron, or a modern worker; but what never vary are the necessities of being in the world, of having to labor and to die there. Accordingly, diverse though human purposes are, none of them are wholly foreign to oneself. "Every purpose, even that of a Chinese, an Indian or a Negro, can be understood by a European. To say it can be understood, means that the European of 1945 may be striving out of a certain situation towards the same limitations in the same way, and that he may re-conceive in himself the purpose of the Chinese, of the Indian or the African."[7]

88

Existentialism, says Sartre, has to start with the Cartesian cogito, and the man who discovers himself directly in the cogito also discovers all the others and discovers them as the condition of his own existence – he cannot *be* anything unless others recognize him as such. "Under these conditions, the intimate discovery I have of myself is at the same time the revelation of the other as a freedom which confronts mine, and which cannot think or will without doing so either for or against me."[8]

Finally, only existentialism is compatible with the dignity of man, being the only philosophy that does not turn him into an object, a "set of pre-determined reactions, in no way different from the patterns of qualities and phenomena which constitute a table, a chair or a stone."

There is something appealing, and even partly convincing, about Sartre's existential humanism. Nevertheless, his critics are probably right in finding it rather theatrical and melodramatic. Also, it does not escape that perennial snare for humanisms: their preoccupation with religion. Sartre's angst is associated by him with "abandonment" – that is to say, abandonment by God. Admittedly, he offers a gloss on this: "When we speak of 'abandonment' – a favourite word of Heidegger – we only mean to say that God does not exist, and that it is necessary to draw the consequences of his absence right to the end." Nevertheless, as a creed, this getting on without God does seem rather reminiscent of what it is replacing.

Also, Sartre's enormous emphasis on *choice,* on Man's "choosing himself" in everything he does, cannot help putting one in mind – not exactly as a refutation, but as a point of reference – of the point Philip Larkin makes unforgettably in "Dockery and Son": that the really decisive factors in our lives are so often exactly the ones we *don't* choose:

> They're more a style
> Our lives bring with them: habit for a while,
> Suddenly they harden into all we've got . . .

8

Antihumanisms

Sartre's *Existentialism Is a Humanism* had widespread re-percussions. Indeed, all the various anti-"humanisms" of the following years seem, in some sense or other, to have taken off from it. Before getting on to that, however, a word is needed about T. E. Hulme, whose *Speculations,* post-humously published in 1924, sparked off a curious and, for a time, very influential anti-"humanist" movement. Hulme's line, broadly speaking, was that the so-called humanism of the Renaissance had been a fatal false step in European thought. It had placed Man rather than God at the center of the stage (Copernicus's discovery having had the opposite effect from what might have been expected), and by doing so it had falsified the relation of the human to the divine. In place of the saving doctrine of original sin, it had enshrined the fatal heresy of the perfectibility of man. From Michelangelo to Rousseauesque humanitarianism and the romantics' dabblings with the infinite, and onward to H. G. Wells and the "flat and insipid optimism of the belief in progress," it had been one continuous slide. The moment had perhaps come, how-ever, for this slide to be reversed. The task of the present age, claimed Hulme, was to abandon the cherished nineteenth-century notion of the *continuity* of reality and face the truth that, just as there is a chasm between the inorganic and the organic, so there is an unbridgeable abyss between the human and the divine.

All along, the center of Hulme's interests was modern (or "modernist") art. He held that there were two possible kinds of art, the "geometrical" and the "vital," and that these were "absolutely distinct in kind from one another" and "created

for the satisfaction of different necessities of the mind." "Geometrical" art was, for him, represented by Byzantine mosaics
and ancient Egyptian sculpture, and he prophesied the re-
emergence of geometrical art in the work of Gaudier-Brzeska
or Wyndham Lewis, as a "precursor of the re-emergence of
the corresponding attitude towards the world," and "the break
up of the Renaissance humanistic attitude."

More broadly, he held that a belief in original sin and the
radical imperfection of man was the very basis of medieval
culture; and of course it was always a weakness in his outlook
that it would be hard to claim that the sculptors at Chartres
Cathedral or St. Trophime, or for that matter Chaucer, were
not profoundly interested in the "human."

This part of his outlook has not worn well. Nevertheless,
Hulme strikes one as an extraordinarily talented thinker, not
easy to sum up. Given his "reactionary" opinions, one might
vaguely have expected him to be an elitist. In fact, he was a
fervent egalitarian, albeit an antidemocratic one, and looked
forward (like Sorel, whom he translated) to a radical trans-
formation of society by revolutionary violence. He was, moreover, to be a major influence on Ezra Pound and Wyndham
Lewis, and he lay behind the bizarre attempt by Hugh Kenner
(a fervent advocate of Pound and Lewis) to represent Joyce's
Ulysses as an anti-"humanist" testament.

Kenner's drift in *Dublin's Joyce* was that Joyce's novel was no
more than a jeering satire on the decline of the West, written from the point of view of medieval Catholicism, and that
Joyce wants Stephen, Bloom, and Molly to be seen, merely, as
pathetic figures of fun. William Empson, reviewing the book,
explained it by reference to American "humanism" in the
Irving Babbitt style. The English, he writes, had not had such a
fierce controversy over "humanism" as Americans had done,
twenty or thirty years ago. "We do not therefore easily realise
that the reason why Bloom, Stephen, Hume, Shelley and so
forth are treated as sub-human by Mr. Kenner is that they
are 'humanists.'" "It strikes me," says Empson, "that the anti-

humanists, now that they are a secure orthodoxy, are over-playing their hand."

Elsewhere, Empson says, teasingly, that it is nice to see Wyndham Lewis express tenderness and admiration for once – even if only about his devil Sammael in *Malign Fiesta*, who forms the idea of "combining the best of the Human Spirit with his Angel's nature." Sammael, of course, has to be shown in the novel to be wrong. "Naturally the spokesman of God had to attack the idea, because T. E. Hulme had said that one must keep the divine and the human absolutely separate, boasting about seducing shopgirls and then boasting about revelation." But it should be remembered, says Empson, that "the Athanasian Creed calls the Incarnation 'the taking of the manhood into God.'"[1]

HEIDEGGER

I come now to the responses to Sartre. There were many of them, and a very striking one was Heidegger's *Letter on Humanism*. On 10 November 1946, a certain Jean Beaufret sent Heidegger a series of queries prompted by Sartre's essay, and Heidegger responded at some length to just one of them: "How can we restore a meaning to the word 'Humanism'?"

He begins by taking Sartre up over the relation of thought to action. Sartrean existentialism holds that man is what he does: he is the sum or result of his actions; and to this Heidegger replies that *thinking* is not to be judged by its results. Thinking has another function: it "lets itself be claimed by Being so that it can say the truth of Being." Its function is the altogether nonutilitarian one of enabling Being to come to Language.

Again, Sartrean existentialism (like Marxism) prescribes political "commitment"; and Heidegger gives his own idiosyncratic gloss on "commitment," which leads on to his fundamental criticism of Western thought. "Thinking," he says – when truly understood – is "commitment *by* Being *for* Being." But maybe, he asks his correspondent, such a statement does not make linguistic sense? Well then, let him simply say,

"Thinking is the commitment *of* Being," allowing the "of" to stand for both possible uses of the genitive – that is to say, "committing Being" and "Being's commitment." This would be natural if language and grammar had not taken a wrong turn almost from the beginning of history. " 'Subject' and 'object' are inappropriate terms of metaphysics, which very early on in the form of Occidental 'logic' and 'grammar' seized control of the interpretation of language. We today can only begin to descry what is concealed in that occurrence."[2]

So, Heidegger asks Beaufret, do we really want to "restore a meaning to the word 'Humanism' "? Do we, indeed, need *any* "isms"? Even such names as "logic," "ethics," and "physics" began to flourish only when truly original thinking, the "thinking of Being," had come to an end and philosophy had begun to be merely a skill or *techne*, a "classroom matter." (The Greeks, during the time of their greatness, were able to think without such "headings.")

Now "humanism," as it has been understood in the past, says Heidegger, belongs to this decadence stage in philosophy. "Humanism," as opposed to "barbarism," is first met with in Rome, as a product of the encounter between Roman civilization and Hellenistic culture (i.e., "classroom education"), and this remained its character during the Renaissance and in the age of Voltaire. "The *humanitas* of *homo humanus* is determined with regard to an already established interpretation of nature, history, world, and the ground of the world, that is of beings as a whole." Thus it actually serves as an obstacle to asking the most important question of all, which concerns "the relation of Being to the essence of man."

The truth is, he says, Aristotle's famous definition of Man as a "rational animal" underestimates the dignity of Man. The gap between Man and the animals is an "abyss," and even the human body is "something essentially other than an animal organism": the "essence" of Man lies elsewhere. Nor is the misconception of man's "essence" remedied by supplementing his body (in Cartesian style) with an immortal soul, or the power of reason, or a personality. The essence of Man lies in his being something more than the "rational animal" of Aristotle and Sartre. He is not "the lord of beings," but "the shepherd of Being."

So – asks Heidegger – ought he, just for the sake of appearances, to retain the name "humanism" for a humanism like his, that contradicts all previous humanisms? Would it not be better to speak openly against "humanism" and risk the malice and misrepresentation that this will bring? He is thinking, evidently, about Nazism and his own relations with the Hitler regime, and he speaks with bitterness of the "logic," or what serves for logic, of those who will accuse him.

Because we speak against "humanism" people fear a defence of the inhuman and a glorification of barbaric brutality. For what is more "logical" than that for somebody who negates humanism nothing remains but the affirmation of inhumanity?

Because we are speaking against "logic" people believe we are demanding that the rigour of thinking be renounced and in its place the arbitrariness of drives and feelings be installed and thus that "irrationalism" be proclaimed as true. For what is more "logical" than that whoever speaks against the logical is defending the alogical?

Because we are speaking against "values" people are horrified at a philosophy that ostensibly dares to despise humanity's best qualities. For what is more "logical" than that a thinking that denies values must necessarily pronounce everything valueless?[3]

LÉVI-STRAUSS

Heidegger's *Letter on Humanism* is an excellent introduction to his thought (Hannah Arendt called it his *Prachtstück*, or masterpiece), but it is hardly very effective as a critique of Sartre. For this we shall have to look elsewhere, and we shall find it in Lévi-Strauss, a formidable opponent both of existentialism and of humanism, whose line of attack on humanism is in many ways the exact opposite of Heidegger's. Far from affirming an "abyss" separating Man from the animals, his aim is a cutting-down-to-size of the "dignity" of man.

In the last chapter of *La Pensée sauvage,* he answers Sartre (the Sartre of the *Critique de la raison dialectique* as well as of *Existentialism Is a Humanism*) at length, accusing him of, among other things, a fatal ethnocentricity. Sartre, he argues, defines Man as a history making animal and thus can hardly bring himself to regard primitive and history-less mankind as possessed of reason, or indeed as properly belonging to humanity at all. Sartre was disconcerted by that native of Ambrym, reported by Deacon, who helpfully explained the marriage regulations and kinship system of his tribe by drawing a diagram in the sand. Sartre would not have it that this native was actually *thinking* analytically, or doing anything more than perform a manual task. Which was perhaps true, remarked Lévi-Strauss, but could equally well be said of an Ecole Polytechnique professor at the blackboard. According to Lévi-Strauss, Sartre was simply indifferent to the "prodigious wealth and diversity of *mores*, beliefs and customs" in the world. "[He has forgotten] that in their own eyes, each of tens and hundreds of thousands of societies which have co-existed on earth, or succeeded one another after man made his appearance there, has taken pride in the conviction – such as we ourselves might entertain – that in itself, be it no more than a little band of nomads or a village deep in the heart of the forest, there was to be found all the meaning and dignity of which human life is capable."[4] They were, of course, mistaken, just as we are liable to be. "It calls for a lot of egocentricity and naivety to believe that the whole of Humanity has taken refuge in one of its historical or geographical modes of being, whereas [a very Lévi-Straussian formulation] *the truth of man lies in the system of their differences and properties in common.*"[5]

Lévi-Strauss challenges the opposition set up by Sartre between dialectic reason, as the one proper to Man, and analytic or "lazy" reason. In reality, Lévi-Strauss argues, the two kinds of reason presuppose each other, and discoveries made by dialectic reason will need to be restated in terms of analytic reason, for that is the language of science. By saying so he is no doubt stamping himself, according to Sartre's vocabulary, as a "transcendental materialist" and an "aesthete" – the kind of man who wants to study humans as though they were ants. But this, says Lévi-Strauss, does not worry him. For one thing, ants, with their elaborate social life and advanced technology, are no easy nut for analysis to crack; and for another, the ultimate aim of the human sciences is not to *constitute* Man but to *dissolve* him. Ethnology is only the first step in a longer process. By empirical study of a great diversity of human societies, it hopes to establish "invariable" features, and may discover them at the most unlikely points. But its next task, having fitted particular humanities into a "general humanity," is to reintegrate human culture into nature, and finally to reintegrate life into physics and chemistry. The ethnologist, that is to say, studies Man not for his own sake but in order to learn something about the world; and that is what is meant by Science.

The brutality of Lévi-Strauss's "dissolve" reminds us, as indeed it is meant to, of the tenderness his writings actually convey toward any species, not excluding the human one. "The diversity of species," he writes in *La Pensée sauvage*, "furnishes man with the most intuitive picture at his disposal and constitutes the most direct manifestation he can perceive of the ultimate discontinuity of reality." To "dissolve," he insists, does not mean to destroy, and the "reductions" of social phenomena that he prescribes become possible only after the phenomena have first been envisaged in all their richness.

The fact remains that, in Lévi-Strauss, we have a conception of Man that could hardly be further removed from Sartre's or Heidegger's. He comes to ethnology with the reductionist conviction, gained from Freud and Marx and the study of geology, that the appearance of things is never going to be their reality. It is a ruling principle with him that the "lived" is not the "real," the "real" being something arrived at by scientific exploration and not available to the everyday human consciousness. "Man" is a fixed and limited creature, whose categorizings of the external world are performed for him by his unconscious mind. Myths "think themselves in men, unknown to them"; and the monotonous similarity of myths shows that the human mind, when not having to grapple with the external world, is "as it were reduced to imitating itself as an object," thus affirming itself to be "a *thing* among other things." (It was, we remember, Sartre's claim that only existentialism was compatible with the dignity of man, being the only philosophy that did not turn him into a thing or object.) A "humanist," clearly, is going to get little encouragement from Lévi-Strauss.

What is to be noticed is that, throughout Lévi-Strauss, pluralism is really the dominant theme. Moreover, it comes in a very attractive form. One can think of few writers so good at suggesting "what it would be like" to be something remote from one's own experience. It is indeed essential to his approach, for in his view, every actual society, whether primitive or civilized, is likely to have something to offer on the question, What form of society is proper to the human species? Rousseau (quite falsely accused of holding that Man could exist outside of society) thought that Neolithic man might have come nearest to the right solution, and Lévi-Strauss is inclined to agree with him: in the Neolithic age, man had already made the largest part of the inventions necessary to his safety (which did not include writing), and he had obtained the leisure to think: "At that age of myth, man was no more free than he is today; but it was merely his humanity that made him a slave. As his authority over nature was very restricted, he found himself protected, and in a sense made free, by the comforting cushion of his dreams."[6]

But it is one thing to imagine pluralistically and quite another to suppose that "pluralism" is a political concept or scheme. Lévi-Strauss has a very striking passage on the subject of overpopulation. It deserves to be quoted at length.

*India attacked this question of numbers 3,000 years ago, seeking by
the caste-system a way of transforming quantity into quality, that is to
say of differentiating human groups in order to allow them to live side
by side. She even conceived the problem in vaster terms: enlarging it
beyond man to all forms of life. The vegetarian regime is inspired by
the same concern as the caste regime – that is to say to prevent social
groups and animal species from treading on each others' toes, to re-
serve to each its own liberty, thanks to a renunciation, on the others'
part, of a rival liberty. It is a tragedy for humankind that this great
experiment failed: I mean that, over the course of history, castes did
not succeed in attaining a condition where they would have remained
equal because different – equal in the sense that they were incommensurable – and that there was introduced among them [my emphasis]*
that perfidious dose of homogeneity which permitted comparison, *and hence the creation of a hierarchy. For if men can succeed
in co-existing on condition that they all regard themselves* equally *as
men, but* differently, *they can also do so by refusing to one another a
comparable degree of humanity, and thus by subordination.*[7]

At a first reading this is very appealing, but on reflection it
strikes one as really most implausible. At least, the caste system as we know it today strikes one as irretrievably and necessarily impregnated with hierarchy – more so indeed than
most social systems. (Though it is a hierarchy expressed not,
as in Europe, in terms of military virtue, or relative armorial
grandeur, but of relative "purity".) Reading this passage, we
remember Lévi-Strauss's cult of Rousseau – Rousseau whose
principle, both in theory and in life, seems to have been that
no one should be expected to have to get on with anybody
else, and who would have nothing to do with any democracy
in which one person "represented" another (which would dis-
qualify almost any democracy feasible today). There is a sort of
contradiction between Lévi-Strauss's skill at seeing members
of other cultures as "like" himself and his rueful phrase about
"that perfidious dose of homogeneity" that allows people to
be compared one with another, and again between the all-

seeing role he claims for the social scientist and the lowly and purblind one he assigns to people like ourselves.

ROLAND BARTHES

In *Le Degré zéro de l'écriture* (1953), Roland Barthes speaks of a new brand of "humanism," one that has "at last integrated History into the image of man." This is the problem for modern writers, and why a modern masterpiece is impossible. To render the "vast freshness" of the present-day world and the awareness of the historically specific image of Man, writers have at their disposal only a "splendid and dead" set of literary conventions, a language formed to express a "timeless essence of man." It is a dilemma, and it is an insoluble one. For their efforts to shed the rituals of literature, and attain a "zero" style or nonstyle, presuppose (what does not yet exist) "an absolutely homogenous condition of society."[8]

Barthes is writing here as a Marxist or neo-Marxist. The text in which Marx most savagely attacks the notion of a "timeless essence of man" is the sixth of his *Theses on Feuerbach*. It runs thus:

Feuerbach resolves the religious essence into the human essence. But the human essence is no abstraction inherent in each single individual. In its reality it is the totality of social relations.

Feuerbach, who does not enter upon a criticism of this real essence, is consequently compelled:

(1) To abstract from the historical process and to fix the religious sentiment as something by itself and to presuppose an abstract – isolated *– human individual.*

(2) The human essence, therefore, can with him be comprehended only as "species," as an inner, mute, general character which merely naturally *unites the many individuals.*[9]

However, if we are to understand Marx's outlook, there is another text that needs to be set beside this one. It is from the *Economic and Philosophical Mss. of 1844:*

Communism as the positive transcendence of private property as human self-estrangement, and therefore as the real appropriation of the human essence by and for man; communism therefore as the complete return of man to himself as a social (i.e. human) being – a return accomplished consciously and embracing the entire wealth of previous development. This communism, as fully developed naturalism, equals humanism, and as fully developed humanism equals naturalism; it is the genuine resolution of the conflict between man and nature and between man and man – the true resolution of the strife between existence and essence, between objectification and self-confirmation, between freedom and necessity, between the individual and the species.[10]

Evidently, in the face of this, one has to admit that Marx was, or at least thought of himself as, a "humanist."

Also, we now get a clearer picture of what he means by the term "species." Under capitalism, he is clearly arguing, man constitutes merely a "natural," or zoological, species; but under communism, he will come into possession of his full "species-being" (a species-being that is intrinsically social, so that his individual life and his species-life will prove one and the same). The drift becomes even clearer if we add the last paragraphs of the first part of *German Ideology*. It would be tempting, Marx says there, to regard medieval "estates," and their successor, "classes," as varieties of the species "man"; but the truth is, human beings are diminished by existing in "estates," and even more so in "classes," which cause them a crippling division between their individual and their "class" existence. "Thus they find themselves directly opposed to the form in which, hitherto, the individuals, of which society consists, have given themselves collective expression, that is, the State. In order, therefore, to assert themselves as individuals, they must overthrow the State."[11]

Marx, then, held that Man had a real essence, or species-being – which makes him not only a humanist but even, it would seem, an "essentialist." But then the thought occurs: to say that "man" has a fixed and unalterable nature, or, alternatively, that human beings are essence-less and decentered products of history, does not really exhaust the possibilities. It will be noticed that Marx speaks of Man's return from his self-estrangement as "embracing the entire wealth of previous development." Evidently, therefore, he did not think of "man" as a mere formless plasma, taking whatever shape material conditions imposed on it. He thought of it, rather, as an organism with its own species-memory and evolutionary continuity. Now, if we think of human beings in this way – that is, as the evolving "human species" – we are not saying that they are unalterable; for, as is well known, species are not permanently fixed.

What is crucial, of course, is that, to adopt Marx's particular brand of humanism, one has to accept the whole communist eschatology and look forward to the abolition of labor and the withering-away of the state; and this is something that, probably, not many of us nowadays are ready to do. Roland Barthes, at any rate, eventually explicitly disowned the Marxist element in *Le Degré zéro de l'écriture* – significantly, in the name of pluralism. In his *Roland Barthes par Roland Barthes* (1975), under the heading "What is a utopia for?" he writes:

In Le Degré zéro de l'écriture *political utopia has the (naive?) form of a social universality, as if utopia could only be the strict converse of the present evil, as if division could only be answered, ultimately, by indivision; but subsequently, though vague and filled with difficulties, a pluralist philosophy has been appearing: hostile to "massification," tending towards difference, in short: Fourierist; whereupon a (still-maintained) utopia consists in imagining an infinitely fragmented society, whose division would no longer be social, and, consequently, no longer conflictive.*[12]

Barthes is still utopian; but his utopia is no longer a Marxist one, that "absolutely homogenous condition of society" in which man realizes his species-being as a social animal, but a pluralist or "Fourierist" one, in which there is no conflict simply because there is no society. "Utopia [à la Fourier]: that of a world in which there would no longer be anything but differences, so that to be differentiated would no longer mean to be excluded." (This is evidently Saussure's view of language, as a system of differences without positive terms, in a new disguise and as an object of yearning.)

As will be seen, "pluralism" here, almost by definition, is not a political concept; and indeed, in his later career, Barthes is visibly depoliticizing himself. He follows out the same set of "pluralistic" thoughts at length in *Sade/Fourier/Loyola* (1971), where he goes out of his way to stress, and praise, the non-sense aspect of Fourier – a thinker who planned, in his utopia, for "thesis meals," where would be debated "the 44 systems of tiny pastries" or "the batches of tiny pastries anathematized by the council"; who decreed that, in his utopia, passions must be changed every two hours; and who solved the problem of the brackishness of seawater by positing "aromal action" by the North Polar cap, which would turn the sea into lemonade. Utopianism, as represented by Barthes, is the direct antithesis of political philosophy. It is a form of pure *writing*, or signifier without a signified: a pure affirmation of desire.

MICHEL FOUCAULT

I come now to perhaps the most formidable of all opponents of humanism. In an interview at the time of the publication of *Les Mots et les choses* (1966), Michel Foucault said: "Our task at the moment is to completely free ourselves from humanism, and in that sense our work is political work."[13] All regimes, both East and West, he explained, "smuggled shoddy goods" under the banner of humanism, and the time had come to denounce all these "mystifications." Later, in a conversation with students in 1971, he defined humanism as "everything in Western civilisation that restricts *the desire for power*," and he described his own goal as being a "desubjectification of the will to power." This could be achieved, he said, by attacking institutions, but also by treating consciousness itself as a field of combat, on which to overthrow "the subject as pseudo-sovereign." Meanwhile, in another of his interviews, he turned the discussion into one about happiness: "We are apparently in the midst of discussing the problem of humanism, but I wonder if in reality we are not in the midst of referring to a much more simple problem, that of happiness. I believe that humanism, at least on the level of politics, might be defined as every attitude that considers the aim of politics to be the production of happiness. Now, I do not think that the notion of happiness is truly thinkable. *Happiness does not exist* – and the happiness of men exists still less." [14]

These are, precisely, statements by the Foucault of the interviews, a somewhat different figure from the writer of *Les Mots et les choses*. So, first of all, one needs to recall what is said in Foucault's *Les Mots et les choses* about "the death of man," an event that, following Nietzsche, he regards as bound up with the "death of God" – and more particularly, what is said there about the *birth* of man.

"Man," he famously argued in *Les Mots et les choses*, is a nineteenth-century invention, a concept that it had been impossible to think in the preceding "classical" episteme. In that episteme – as in Velasquez's painting *Las Meninas* – the sovereign subject (Man), the focus of all representations, had to stay out of the picture. Matters were otherwise with the entity known as "human nature." The concept of "human nature," he contended, was at home in the classical episteme. "And if it is objected that no epoch attributed more significance to 'human nature' or gave it a firmer, more definitive and more articulate status, one can reply that the very concept of human nature, and the manner in which it functioned, excluded the possibility of a 'science of man.' " [15] It was only in the nineteenth century that Man himself became an object for gaze; and it was to study Man, an ambiguous figure at once an object of knowledge and a knowing subject, that the "human sciences" (anthropology, psychology, and cultural history) were born. Foucault's point here seems a very good one. It expresses, for one thing, the sense of imprisonment one gets from the unalterable "human nature" purveyed by Molière and La Bruyère and classic moralists of their type.

As for the "death of man": Foucault's attitude in *Les Mots et les choses* is that (like the Second Coming) it may happen at any moment and perhaps soon, but at all events it is warmly to be desired. Philosophy since Kant has fallen into an "anthropological sleep" from which it is time it awakened.

To all those who wish to go on talking about man, his reign or his liberation, to all those who still pose questions about the essence of man, to all those who want to take him as a starting-point in the pursuit of truth, to all those who, conversely, refer back all truths to man himself, to all those who do not want to [formalize] without anthropologising, who do not want to mythologise without demystifying, who do not want to think without immediately thinking that it is man who is thinking, to all these clumsy and warped [gauches et gauchies] forms of reflection one can only reply with a philosophic laugh – that is to say, in a certain part, a silent one.[16]

That we ought to wish for the "death of man" is important in Foucault's outlook, and he seems to have believed that this event could be hastened by accomplishing the death of the self or "Subject." In contradistinction from Sartre, who downgraded the concept of "we," representing it as a mere ghost of an "I," Foucault made it his business to unsettle the concept of "I." This overthrowing of the "I" or "Subject as pseudo-sovereign" would require "treating consciousness itself as a field of combat," and, by implication, it would be a political activity – a branch, no doubt, of "politics of the person."

In Foucault's personal life, as is well known, to get rid of the self, to *"se déprendre de soi-même"* [lose one's fondness for oneself] and have no identity or *état civil*, was an obsession. To the imaginary interlocutor in *L'Archéologie du savoir*, who asks him if it is a deliberate ploy of his always to spring up somewhere *else*, nowhere near where his readers expect to find him, he replies: "I am no doubt not the only one who writes in order to have no face." In the spirit of his "What is an Author?"

he would have liked not to have to be the author of his own works; and in his inaugural lecture at the Collège de France he said he wished he could "slip unnoticed into his discourse and be "situated at random within its unfolding." In the same spirit, he once told a bemused interviewer: "I do not say things because I think them. I say them rather with the aim of self-destruction, so that I will not have to think them any more, so that I can be certain that from now on they will live a life outside me, or die the death in which I will not have to recognize myself."[17]

On the question of the Self he was really very consistent. It was part of his objection to Sartre that the concept of "authenticity" smuggled back the obfuscating notion of a "true" self. "Sartre avoids the idea of the self as something which is given to us," he said, "but through the moral notion of 'authenticity' he returns to the idea that we have to be ourselves – to be truly our true self."[18] The Californian cult of the self struck him as childish; and in his Howison lectures, delivered at Berkeley in 1980, he sounded a quasi-Christian and Pascalian note. "No truth about the self is without the sacrifice of the self."

The point is important when it comes to Foucault as a political theorist. His political objection to humanism, as has been seen, was that it represented "everything in Western civilisation that restricts the desire for power." Humanism was the hypocrisy exemplified in social historians, who liked to represent the popular insurrections of the past as arising from famine, taxes, or unemployment – from anything save a desire for power. Foucault's drastic formula takes the "liberal humanist" aback; but the sting is somewhat taken out of it by the fact that what he is calling for is a "de-subjectification" of the will to power. Thus we are not meant to spell his formula out in terms of interest-politics, or a Hobbesian "war of every man against every man," but to think of power, rather, as the tissue or chemical building block of all cultural phenomena, and as such morally neutral. According to this theory, the forces possessed by the body to resist power are the result of the exercise of power and discipline *on* it.

Admittedly, Foucault is not a very consistent political thinker. He is liable, when it suits him, to invoke the archaic notion of human "rights." Remarks here and there, too, suggest that in fact he regarded all exercises of power as "intolerable" – an epithet he was fond of using.

It remains to consider his charge against humanism, that "it might be defined as every attitude that considers the aim of politics to be the production of happiness." One's instinctive response is that, partly at least, he is quite right, if not altogether in the sense he is intending. For it is surely true that political theory ought not to regard its aim as being to produce happiness, but rather, merely, to remedy unhappiness. It seems absurd (though utopian thinkers have persisted in doing it) to form theories about what will make people happy, for happiness has to be invented by the individual. Happiness is supererogatory. One can always say, "I may be very fortunate, but I am not happy." (The negative theory of politics, it is worth adding, cuts through a lot of problems. It renders unnecessary much quite fruitless debate, on the pattern of "Is it right to combat social inequalities, seeing that perfect equality, if you ever achieved it, would be stifling?")

As to there being no such thing as happiness, though, the humanist – one feels it strongly – is bound not to agree. It has not been proved yet that we need "humanism," but here, at least, seems to be a feature to be added to its concept. A humanist has to believe in happiness, and is in fact a product of a period in history that distinguishes conscious happiness from mere good fortune.

But further, to be able to say "I am happy," it seems as if one will have to be willing, as Foucault was not, to say "I." In Foucault's scheme, the place of happiness is taken by "pleasure," especially self-extinguishing pleasures. One has here a neat way of confronting the antihumanist Foucault with a persuasive exponent of humanism, E. M. Forster. For it was Forster's message in *Howards End,* or part of it – the doctrine of "only connect" – that one should aspire to possess oneself as a whole and to live in the moment and that this meant belonging with those who can say "I." By contrast: "No superman ever said 'I want.' Because 'I want' must lead to the question, 'Who am I?' and so to Pity and to Justice. He only says 'want.'" Similarly, according to Forster, the "business" mind was incapable of saying "I," the place where "I" should be, being filled with "panic and emptiness."[19] Forster, moreover, regarded it as a duty to recognize happiness, and to attach significance to it if it should happen to come. In the year 1932 he made an entry in his *Commonplace Book:*

Happiness
I have been happy for two years.
It mayn't be over yet, but I want to write it down before it gets spoiled by pain – which is the chief thing pain can do in the inside life: spoil the lovely things that had got in there first. Happiness can come in one's natural growth and not queerly, as religious people think. From 51 to 53 I have been happy, and would like to remind others that their turn can come too. It is the only message worth giving.[20]

If Foucault is right that "Man" was only invented in the nineteenth century, one might perhaps say, with a touch of exaggeration, that something like this is also true of happiness. The classical world, certainly, seems to have recognized no distinction between "happy "and "fortunate," and Solon's "Call no man happy until he is dead," though no doubt intended as a paradox, was not the one we are sometimes tempted to think it. By the eighteenth century in Britain the distinction had, in a sense, been recognized, and the word "happiness" could be used to denote not only "good fortune" but a state of mind. However, in this secondary and still subordinate sense it was still usual to link it closely with some particular cause of happiness or some recipe for it. ("Happiness *is* . . . so-and-so: it is pleasure, or cultivating one's garden.") The note is particularly clear in Samuel Johnson: "There is nothing which has yet been contrived by man, by which so much happiness is produced as by a good tavern"; or "Were it not for imagination, Sir, a man would be as happy in the arms of a chambermaid as of a Duchess."

One senses, therefore, that a fresh step has been taken when Blake writes to William Hayley (7 October 1803), "Please to pay for me my best thanks to Miss Poole, tell her that I wish her a continued Excess of Happiness – some say that Happiness is not good for Mortals, and they ought to be answer'd that Sorrow is not fit for Immortals and is utterly useless to any one." The key word here is "Excess." Blake seems to be picturing a free-floating happiness, independent of any direct cause. The same notion is implied when he writes: "With happiness stretch'd across the hills," or in the unbidden happiness evoked in his "Nurse's Song," and it becomes, increasingly, a leading sense of "happiness." "Happiness" is to be distinguished from "joy," in that, to "joy," it adds some notion of finding the world good. In a world filled with appalling suffering, this makes it easy to dismiss it as criminally selfish and pharisaic. Here Blake, who dared to lay claim to personal happiness, is exemplary, for no one has better analyzed the dilemmas entailed by this claim. His "Pity would be no more / If we did not make somebody Poor; / And Mercy no more could be / If all were as happy as we" takes us deep into the same questions as Wittgenstein's "Only a very unhappy man has the right to pity others."

The development of the notion of "happiness" seems to have been linked to what Lionel Trilling once described, in a famous essay, as "The fate of pleasure" [21] – that is to say, the revulsion against "pleasure" in the nineteenth century as a word that had got into bad company. When Carlyle repudiates the Benthamite calculus of pains and pleasures as a "Pig-philosophy"; when Dostoevsky's "Underground man" rejects pleasure in favor of the gratifications of unpleasure, as more in accord with the dignity and freedom of man – it marks, according to Trilling, a major turn in Western high culture, leading to the divorce of high art and progressive politics. In the gap that this left there has grown up a more exact and more imaginative conception of "happiness." It seems a kind of corroboration for this idea that a particularly magnificent and compelling evocation of happiness, Philip Larkin's "Wedding-Wind," was composed by someone who considered happiness quite out of the question for himself.

9
Politics, New Style and Old

I n this book I have mentioned a number of traits that might help to define a humanist. A humanist would hold that, in theory at least, one could imagine what it would be "like" to be any other kind of human being. He or she would believe themselves to contain the whole human potential and dislike all attempts at splitting up the human psyche, the positing of distinct human "kinds" or "breeds," or taking pride, or encouraging others to take pride, in "difference." A humanist would be attentive to the question, What can or cannot be said from a given human position (and what can or can't be *seen* from a given position). A humanist would believe in the objectivity of "value" and would suppose that the world contains a great diversity of intrinsically valuable things.

It has still to be considered, though, what would be the point of calling oneself a humanist: why it would be necessary to affirm humanism as a doctrine. Actually, it has probably never been a good idea to envisage humanism as a *movement*. There is, after all, no necessity to get together with others in order to think. Numbers and togetherness ought not to count in humanism (just as it is an error for liberals or pragmatists to represent themselves as a phantom horde or united battalion). To be a humanist, anyway of my kind, should really require no more than solitary introspection.

The strongest motive for adopting the label seems, in fact, to be a natural and well-grounded resistance to anti-"humanism." It is a resistance that most of all comes home to one – to me, anyway – in regard to literature, and some works of literature that I especially admire. What these works are grappling with, with great earnestness, is the danger of dehumanization.

This is the specter, in the guise of aestheticism, that haunted Henry James, who feared its presence in his own self. Running all through *The Portrait of a Lady* is the unspoken implication that, in Gilbert Osmond's view, Isabel is merely another "thing" (of the "best kind") to add to his collection. Equally, dehumanization is the theme of Joyce's unforgettable story "A Painful Case," in *Dubliners*. Its hero, Mr. Duffy, has managed to petrify and depersonalize his existence, encasing it in "taste" and habit. "He lived at a little distance from his body, regarding his own acts with doubtful side-glances. He had an odd autobiographical habit which led him to compose in his mind from time to time a short sentence about himself containing a subject in the third person and a predicate in the past tense." The fate that lies in store for this willing victim of dehumanization, and even more for the woman he allows to involve herself with him, is almost unbearably poignant. I think, too, of the devastating last sentence of Kafka's *Metamorphosis,* where we read how Gregor's sister, in confirmation of her parents' "new dreams and excellent intentions" of finding her a good husband, "sprang to her feet . . . and stretched her young body." We realize that it is she, not Gregor, who is being envisaged as a beetle.

It is a related thought that the attack on "essentialism," when applied too rigidly to literature, can land up in sheer paradox. I am thinking of Jonathan Dollimore's *Radical Tragedy,* a study of Elizabethan and Jacobean drama.[1] Dollimore holds that "essentialist humanism" has been the fatal failing of English literary criticism. It may take a Christian form, or an "ethical" or secular form, or an existentialist form, but ultimately these derive from the same metaphysical mode of thought – designed to mystify suffering and smooth out contradictions and discontinuities in the name of an unreal harmony. These plays, he argues, and *King Lear* among them, look forward rather to Brecht's "epic theater": a theater (to use Walter Benjamin's words) that presents an "untragic hero" who is "like an empty stage on which the contradictions of our society are acted out" – one that dispenses with empathy and in which "actors *show* rather than *become* the characters they play."

The trouble with this is that, at bottom, it implies that Shakespeare does not mean the spectator to be moved by Lear and his fate – a proposition that hardly makes sense. The notion would have weight, really, only on the assumption that all tragedy had to be Brechtian and that the spectator must *never* feel for, or entertain a fellow feeling with, a character in a drama or a novel. (That certain Victorian novelists encouraged their readers in a day-dreaming *identification* with their heroes or heroines is of course a different matter.) Humanism has to assume that, in imagination, one can put oneself in another's shoes. But this in turn presupposes that "man" possesses, if not an "essence," at least a historical continuity, so that one might, not absurdly, feel a fellowship with Shakespeare's Lear, as he, on the heath, is enabled to do with "Poor naked wretches."

The declared objective of anti-"humanism," according to Dollimore, is the "de-centring of man." The phrase combines two senses: dislodging Man from the center of the universe; and, more importantly, dissolving the human Subject – federalizing it, "pluralizing" it, freeing "Man" from the need for a center. Here lies the force of Lacan's campaign against American-type "ego-psychology." Any "unity" attributed to the ego, according to Lacan, must be spurious, the self or Subject being (like language, according to Saussure) an articulation of difference. As Malcolm Bowie paraphrases him, "The other-infested subject can have no other destiny than that of successive disappearance and return, entity and non-entity, sense and nonsense, concentration and dispersal, being there and being gone."[2] It is in this spirit that Foucault aspires to live "dispersed" and that Barthes writes: "Today the subject apprehends himself *elsewhere,* and 'subjectivity' can return at another place on the spiral: deconstructed, taken apart, shifted, without anchorage: why should I not speak of 'myself' since this 'my' is no longer 'the self?'"[3]

This repudiation of unity, one perceives, is a defence strategy. The underlying assumption is that one is safer, less exposed to domination, if one does not have an "I" or civic identity – is not to be found in the place where people or the authorities expect. The postmodernist attitude toward the "I" is altogether political, in the "politics of the person" sense of the word.

Here we meet with one of the formidable paradoxes besetting "politics of the person." For there seems to be a kind of antithesis between regarding oneself as decentered (dispersed, multiple in one's identity) and claiming influence in virtue of being *one* thing – a woman, or black, or gay, or whatever. (Dollimore frankly admits that, taken to its full length, antihumanism might appear to rule out all political action. For if "man or the "subject" is completely dispersed, he, it, or she must become incapable of acting as an agent, "least of all as an agent of change.")

Earlier I touched on another of the paradoxes of "politics of the person," or at least a fundamental difficulty: that there seems to be no way in which taking pride in one's difference is not going to be damaging to one's neighbors. (No political system so far conceived, or perhaps conceivable, is able to prevent it.)

Both paradoxes say something about the nature of "politics of the person." One has to be careful not to confuse "politics of the person" (politics not concerned with a polis) with traditional humanitarian politics. It retains within it relics of traditional politics, but not of the domestic but of the international or "balance of power" kind. Its habit is to create around itself an aura of diplomatic relations, frontier incidents, chauvinism, and irredentism – which is what prompts certain philosophers to volunteer for the part of peacekeeper, a dubious and self-congratulatory role.

My argument ends at this point. In this book I have harped

a good deal on philanthropy, and the reason should be plain. For the great strength, or apparent strength, of "politics of the person" (politics without a polis) is that it is free from the taint of philanthropy; but there is a high price to pay for this – no less than that of involving the term "politics" in self-contradiction. It seems, then, that it is no substitute for traditional politics (or, as you might call it, "politics proper"); and this form of politics is by nature on behalf of someone or something not itself. It is, so far as I can see, incurably philanthropic; and being so, it is exposed to all the snares and temptations with which philanthropy is plagued.

Notes

1. A RULE OF BEHAVIOR

1. Ludwig Wittgenstein, *Culture and Value*, ed. G. H. Von Wright (London: Blackwell, 1980), p.30e.
2. Leo Tolstoy, *What Then Must We Do?* trans. Aylmer Maude (London: Oxford University Press, 1925), p.57.
3. Tolstoy, *What Then Must We Do?* p.45.

2. "PLURALISM"

1. Isaiah Berlin, *Vico and Herder* (London: Hogarth, 1976), p.153.
2. Bernard Williams, *Moral Luck* (Cambridge: Cambridge University Press, 1981), p.72.
3. Williams, *Moral Luck*, p.77.
4. *Plutarch's Lives*, ed. Ernest Rhys (London: Dent, 1910), 1:492.
5. Berlin, *Vico and Herder*, p.211.
6. Perry Anderson, "England's Isaiah," *London Review of Books*, 20 December 1990, 6.
7. Claude Lévi-Strauss, *Tristes tropiques* (Paris: Plon, 1955), p.347. Unless otherwise noted, all translations are my own.
8. Berlin, *Vico and Herder*, p.211.
9. Quoted by Ernest Gellner in *Culture, Identity, and Politics* (Cambridge: Cambridge University Press, 1987), p.58.

3. "WE," "US," AND "I"

1. Shakespeare, *Coriolanus*, act 1, scene 1.
2. Plato, *Republic*, trans. Alexander Dunlap Lindsay (London: Dent, 1935), book 4, p.130.
3. Jean-Paul Sartre, *L'Etre et le néant* (Paris: Gallimard, 1943), p.474.
4. Jean-Paul Sartre, *La Nausée* (Paris: Gallimard, 1938), pp.153–54.
5. Richard Rorty, *Contingency, Irony and Solidarity* (Cambridge: Cambridge University Press, 1989), p.198.
6. D. H. Lawrence, *Studies in Classic American Literature* (1923; reprint, London: Heinemann, 1964), p.155.

4. RACE AND NATIONALISM

1. P. N. Furbank, *Unholy Pleasure: the Idea of Social Class* (New York: Oxford University Press, 1985), chapter 1.
2. Ellis Horell Minns, *Enyclopaedia Britannica,* 11th ed., s.v. "Slavs."
3. Homi K. Bhabha, *The Location of Culture* (London: Routledge, 1994), p.4.
4. *Social Text* (fall 1986).
5. See Aijaz Ahmad, "Jameson's Rhetoric of Otherness and the 'National Allegory,'" in his *In Theory: Classes, Nations, Literatures* (London: Verso, 1992), pp.95–122.
6. Ernest Gellner, *Nations and Nationalism* (London: Blackwell, 1983).
7. Noel Malcolm, *Bosnia: A Short History* (reprint, New York: New York University Press, 1996), p.197.
8. Malcolm, *Bosnia,* p.199.
9. Julian Sorell Huxley and A. C. Haddon, *We Europeans: A Survey of "Racial" Problems* (London: Jonathan Cape, 1935), p.136.

5. BEHALF

1. Mark Girouard, *Return to Camelot* (New Haven: Yale University Press, 1981), p.68.
2. Quoted in Graham Wallas, *The Life of Francis Place* (London: Longman, 1898), p.72.
3. Harold Perkin, *The Origins of Modern English Society 1780–1880* (London: Routledge, 1969), p.258.
4. Henrietta Barnett, *Canon Barnett: His Life, Work and Friends* (London: Murray, 1918), 1:34.
5. Lionel Trilling, *The Liberal Imagination* (New York: Doubleday, 1950), p.214.
6. Karl Marx, *The Poverty of Philosophy* (1847), in *Collected Works,* (London: Lawrence & Wishart, 1976), 6:177.
7. Quoted in Alan Sheridan, *Michel Foucault: The Will to Truth* (London: Tavistock, 1980), p.114.
8. Quoted in K. A. Reader, *Intellectuals and the Left in France since 1968* (London: Macmillan, 1987), pp.10–11.
9. John Fekete, *The Critical Twilight* (London: Routledge, 1971).
10. Marx, *German Ideology* (1845), in *Collected Works* (1976), 5:60.
11. *Roland Barthes by Roland Barthes,* trans. R. Howard (London: Macmillan, 1977), p.85.
12. Sheridan, *Michel Foucault,* p.113.
13. Edward Said, *Culture and Imperialism* (London: Chatto & Windus, 1993), pp.407–8.

14. *London Review of Books,* 13 February 1992, pp.16–17.
15. Gerard Manley Hopkins, *Letters of Gerard Manley Hopkins to Robert Bridges,* ed. C. C. Abbott (London: Oxford University Press, 1935), p.83.

6. THE POLITICS OF GENDER

1. Claude Lévi-Strauss, *Les Structures élémentaires de la parenté* (Paris: Presses Universitaires de France, 1949), p.175.
2. Christine di Stefano, "Dilemmas of Difference," in *Feminism/Postmodernism,* ed. Linda J. Nicholson (London: Routledge, 1990), p.64.
3. Di Stefano, "Dilemmas," p.66.
4. *Radical Philosophy* no. 59 (autumn 1991): 3–14.

7. HUMANISMS

1. T. S. Eliot, *Selected Essays* (London: Faber & Faber, 1932), p.473.
2. David James Fisher, *Romain Rolland and the Politics of Intellectual Engagement* (Berkeley: University of California Press, 1988), p.227.
3. Fisher, *Romain Rolland,* 221.
4. M. Merleau-Ponty, *Humanisme et terreur* (Paris: Gallimard, 1947), p.129.
5. Michel Tournier, *The Wind Spirit,* trans. A. Goldhammer (London: Collins, 1989), pp.132–33.
6. Jean-Paul Sartre, *Existentialism and Humanism,* trans. P. Mairet (London: Methuen, 1948), p.55.
7. Sartre, *Existentialism and Humanism,* p.46.
8. Sartre, *Existentialism and Humanism,* p.45.

8. ANTIHUMANISMS

1. William Empson, "The Cult of Unnnaturalism," in *Argufying,* ed. J. Haffenden (London: Chatto & Windus, 1987), pp.628–29.
2. Martin Heidegger, *Basic Writings,* ed. D. F. Krell, rev. ed. (San Francisco: Harper, 1993), p.218.
3. Heidegger, *Basic Writings,* p.249.
4. C. Lévi-Strauss, *La Pensée sauvage* (Paris: Plon, 1962), p.329.
5. Lévi-Strauss, *La Pensée sauvage,* p.329.
6. Lévi-Strauss, *Tristes tropiques,* p.352.
7. Lévi-Strauss, *Tristes tropiques,* p.128.
8. Roland Barthes, *Le Degré zéro de l'écriture* (Paris: Gonthier, 1953), pp.73–74.

9. *The Marx-Engels Reader,* ed. R. C. Tucker, 2nd ed. (New York: Norton, 1978), p.145.

10. Marx, *Collected Works* (1975), 3:296.

11. *The Marx-Engels Reader,* p.200.

12. *The Marx-Engels Reader,* p.77.

13. Quoted in David Macey, *The Lives of Michel Foucault* (London: Hutchinson, 1993), p.171.

14. Interview by James Miller, 1967, in Miller, *The Passion of Michel Foucault* (New York: Simon & Schuster, 1993), p.173.

15. Michel Foucault, *Les Mots et les choses* (Paris: Gallimard, 1966), p.320.

16. Foucault, *Les Mots et les choses,* pp.353–54.

17. Quoted in Miller, *The Passion of Michel Foucault,* p.240.

18. See Macey, *The Lives of Michel Foucault,* p.458.

19. E. M. Forster, *Howards End* (London: Edward Arnold, 1910), chapter 4.

20. E. M. Forster, *Commonplace Book,* ed. Philip Gardner (London: Scolar, 1985), p.94.

21. Lionel Trilling, "The Fate of Pleasure," in *Beyond Culture* (Harmondsworth, England: Penguin, 1966).

9. POLITICS, NEW STYLE AND OLD

1. Jonathan Dollimore, *Radical Tragedy* (London: Harvester, 1984).

2. Malcolm Bowie, *Lacan* (London: Fontana, 1991), p.82.

3. Barthes, *Barthes by Barthes,* p.168.

Index

abandonment, 89
Achebe, Chinua, 47
aestheticism, 112
agnosticism, 83
Ahmad, Aijaz, 47
AIDS, 69–70
altruism, 57–58
anarchy, 67
Anderson, Benedict: *Imagined Communities*, 48
Anderson, Perry, 17
Antigone, 12
antihumanism, 83, 91–110, 111, 113–14
anti-Semitism, 40
Aquinas, St. Thomas, 86
Arendt, Hannah, 95
Aristides, 15
Aristotle, 14–16, 20, 34, 94–95; *Politics*, 34–36
Arnold, Matthew, 61
Aron, Raymond: *Opium of the Intellectuals*, 86
art: Hulme on, 91–92
atheism, 83
Augustine, Saint, 75
Austro-Hungarian Empire, 22

Babbitt, Irving, 84–85, 92
Balzac, Honoré de, 44
Barnett, Henrietta, 59
Barnett, Canon Samuel Augustus, 62
Barthes, Roland, 67, 83, 113; *Le Degré zéro de l'écriture*, 100, 102; *Roland Barthes par Roland Barthes*, 102; *Sade/Fourier/Loyola*, 103

Beaufret, Jean, 93–94
Beauvoir, Simone de: *Le Deuxième sexe*, 73
behalf: defined, 57
Benjamin, Walter, 112
Bentham, Jeremy, 109
Berlin, Isaiah: defines pluralism, 11–13, 16–17, 20; *The Crooked Timber of Humanity*, 17; *Vico and Herder*, 16–17, 22
Bhabha, Homi K., 46
Blake, William, 109
Booth, Charles, 7
Booth, William, 7
Bordo, Susan: "Feminism, Postmodernism and Gender-Scepticism," 78
Borges, Jorge Luis, 47
Bosnia, 52–53, 55
Bradley, Francis Herbert, 84
Brecht, Bertolt, 112–13
Bridges, Robert, 71
Britain. *See* Labour movement
Bunyan, John: *Pilgrim's Progress*, 6
Byron, George Gordon, 6th Baron, 46

Campbell, Gordon, 36
Carlyle, Thomas, 109
Carroll, Lewis, 46
caste system (India), 35, 99
Cecil, Edgar Algernon Gascoyne-Cecil, Viscount, 58
charity, 3, 6
Chaucer, Geoffrey, 92
chivalry, 58
Christian Socialism, 57

class (social), 27, 41, 58, 60–61, 65, 101
Cocteau, Jean: *Round the World in 80 Hours*, 87
"color" (human), 75–76
commitment, 93–94
communism: and humanism, 38, 85–86, 101–2
Comte, Auguste, 2, 87
Conrad, Joseph: *The Nigger of the Narcissus*, 1
Croats, 52–53
culture: ethnographers' views of, 17–20; and pluralism, 11–12, 16–17, 25

Deacon, Arthur Bernard, 96
Deleuze, Gilles, 64
Deniker, J., 41–43
despotism, 22–23
Dickens, Charles, 59
di Stefano, Christine: "Dilemmas of Difference," 76–80
Dollimore, Jonathan: *Radical Tragedy*, 112–14
Dostoevsky, Fedor, 109
Duckworth, Wynfrid Laurence Henry, 43
Durkheim, Emile, 29

Einstein, Albert, 14
Eliot, T. S.: "The Humanism of Irving Babbitt," 85
emotivism, 14
Empson, William, 92–93
engagement, 86
Engels, Friedrich, 60
Enright, Dennis Joseph: "The Noodle-Vendor's Flute," 4–6
essentialism, 112–13
estates (social), 28, 101
ethnic: as term, 54–55. *See also* race
ethnocentrism, 33–34
ethnographers, 17–20
ethnology, 97

European Community, 52
existentialism, 86–89, 93, 101

Fekete, John, 66
feminism: and gender differences, 73–82; and rationalism, 79; and social justice, 59; writings and audience, 73–74
feudalism, 51
Feuerbach, Ludwig Andreas, 100
Finn, Huckleberry (fictional character), 12, 32–33
Forster, Edward Morgan, 27, 107–8; *Commonplace Book*, 108; *Howards End*, 108; *A Passage to India*, 51
Foucault, Michel: antihumanism of, 83, 103–10, 113; on gender and human identity, 76; influence on 1968 Paris "events," 64; *L'Archéologie du savoir*, 105; *Les Mots et les choses*, 103–5; "What is an Author?" 105
Fourier, François Marie Charles, 67, 102–3
Freud, Sigmund: and "oceanic feeling," 86
friendship: clash with justice, 15–16

Gaudier-Brzeska, Henri, 92
gay identity (homosexuality), 69–70, 76
Gay Times (magazine), 69
Gellner, Ernest, 22, 48–51
gender. *See* sex
generations, 36, 39
Girouard, Mark: *Return to Camelot*, 58
Gladstone, William Ewart, 58, 60–61
Glaucon, 26, 35
God: and concept of humanity, 30; and human abandonment, 89; and humanism, 91
Green, John Richard, 41

Guizot, François Pierre Guillaume, 44

Gunn, Thom: *The Man With Night Sweats*, 69

Haddon, A. C., 43, 54
happiness, 104, 107–10
Haraway, Donna: "A Manifesto for Cyborgs," 78
Hayley, William, 109
Heaney, Seamus, 70
heaven: Swedenborg on, 25
Hegel, Georg Wilhelm Friedrich, 28, 39, 50
Heidegger, Martin, 83, 89, 97; *Letter on Humanism*, 93–94
Herder, Johann Gottfried von, 11, 16–17, 20–23; *Yet Another Philosophy of History*, 20
Hill, Octavia, 59
Himmelfarb, Gertrude: *The Idea of Poverty*, 6; *Poverty and Compassion*, 6
Hinduism: caste theory, 35, 99
history: philosophy of, 39–40
Hitler, Adolf, 95
Hobbes, Thomas, 16, 106; *Leviathan*, 26–27
Holocaust, 2
homosexuality. *See* gay identity
Hopkins, Gerard Manley, 71
Hulme, T. E.: *Speculations*, 91–93
humanism: belief in value of, 111; and communism, 38, 85–86, 101–2; and concept of objective "us," 30; and feminism, 79–80; Foucault rebuts, 103–10; and happiness, 107; Heidegger on, 93–95; and history, 40; and imagination, 3; and individual, 1–2, 23, 38, 40, 111; in literature, 111–13; movements and exponents, 83–89; and philanthropy, 61; and religion, 83–84, 89; and right to judge, 2–6; Sartre on, 30–31, 86–89, 93. *See also* antihumanism

humanity: and individual, 11, 29–30, 38–40; religion of, 2
Hume, David, 92
Huxley, Julian Sorell, and A. C. Haddon: *We Europeans*, 54

ideals: incompatibility of, 11–13, 16–17, 20–21
imagination: and humanism, 3–4; and moral choice, 12
imperialism, 68–69
India: caste system in, 35, 99
individuality: and human solidarity, 1, 23, 36; and human species, 11, 29, 39–40; and the state, 27
industrialization, 48–50

James, Henry: *The Portrait of a Lady*, 112
James, William, 84
Jameson, Frederic: "Third World Literature in the Era of Multinational Capitalism," 47
Jews: deprived of rights, 52. *See also* anti-Semitism
Johnson, Samuel, 108; *Dictionary*, 54
Jonson, Ben, 70
Joyce, James: "A Painful Case," 112; *Portrait of the Artist as a Young Man*, 38; *Ulysses*, 92
justice: clash with friendship, 15–16; and philanthropic outsider, 59

Kafka, Franz: *Metamorphosis*, 112
Kant, Immanuel, 12, 23, 33, 51, 105
Kenner, Hugh: *Dublin's Joyce*, 92
Kipling, Rudyard, 36
Kipling Society, 20

labor: division of, 35
Labour movement (Britain), 66–67

La Bruyère, Jean de, 105
Lacan, Jacques, 65, 113
Larkin, Philip: "Dockery and Son," 89; "Wedding-Wind," 110
Lawrence, D. H., 1, 23, 36, 39; *The Crown*, 37; "Everlasting Flowers for a Dead Mother," 37; *The Rainbow*, 36–37; *Women in Love*, 36–37
Lenin, Vladimir I., 60
Lévi-Strauss, Claude: antihumanism of, 83, 95–100; on biological contrasts, 74; and Indian caste system, 98–99; *La Pensée sauvage*, 96, 97; *Tristes tropiques*, 17–20
Lewis, Wyndham, 92–93; *Malign Fiesta*, 93
liberal democracy, 22–23
liberal humanism, 31
literacy: and industrial society, 48
London Review of Books, 65
Loyola, St. Ignatius, 103
Lu Xun, 47

MacIntyre, Alasdair: *After Virtue*, 14–15
Malcolm, Noel: *Bosnia: A Short History*, 52–53
Malinowski, Bronislaw, 22
Malraux, André, 86
Mann, Tom, 58
Maritain, Jacques: *Humanisme intégral*, 86
Marx, Karl: and class, 67; on communism as humanism, 38, 101–2; and loss of humanity, 2; on philanthropy, 60–61, 64; *Contribution to the Critique of Hegel's "Philosophy of Law,"* 28; *Economic and Philosophical Mss. of 1844*, 100; *The Eighteenth Brumaire*, 60; *German Ideology*, 66; *The Poverty of Philosophy*, 60; *Theses on Feuerbach*, 100
Marxism, 64, 79, 86–87, 93, 100

May events (1968). *See* Paris
McMillan, Carol, 80
Mearns, Andrew: *The Bitter Cry of Outcast London*, 7
Merleau-Ponty, Maurice: *Humanisme et terreur*, 85
Michelangelo Buonarroti, 91
Mill, James, 58
Mill, John Stuart, 46
Minns, E. H., 43
Molière (Jean Baptiste Poquelin), 105
monadism, 34, 39
moral values: conflict of, 12–17, 21; nonabsolute, 33; and "we-consciousness," 32–33
More, Paul Elmer, 84
Muslims: in Bosnia, 53
myth, 98

Nagel, Thomas: *Mortal Questions*, 13
Naipaul, Sir V. S., 47
nation: and belonging, 28; and race, 52; and territory, 51. *See also* state, the
nationalism, 34, 45–51
natural man, 19, 25
Nazism, 95
neo-Hegelianism, 84
Nicholson, Linda: *Feminism/Postmodernism* (symposium), 76–77
Nietzsche, Friedrich, 16, 104
Nott, Josiah Clark, and George Robins Gliddon: *Types of Mankind*, 44

Oakeshott, Michael, 16, 20
O'Connell, Daniel, 58
original sin, 92
Orwell, George, 46
Ottoman Empire, 22
overpopulation, 98–99

Pan-Slavism, 45

Paris: May 1968 "events," 57, 64–66, 68

Perkin, Harold: *The Origins of Modern English Society 1780–1880*, 58

philanthropy, 32, 57–63, 67, 71, 115

pity, 6–7, 9

Place, Francis, 68

Plato, 15, 26, 35, 84; *Republic*, 35

pleasure, 109. *See also* happiness

pluralism: Barthes on, 103; Isaiah Berlin defines, 11–12, 16–17, 23; and despotism, 22–23; Herder on, 21–23; Lévi-Strauss extols, 98; and moral confusion, 14; as political concept, 23, 25, 67; and "politics of the person," 67; and postmodernism, 80

Plutarch, 15

political theory: and actual society, 20

"politics of the person" ("politics of difference"), 57, 64–70, 82, 114–15

Positivism, 2

postmodernism: and feminism, 76–80

Pound, Ezra, 92

poverty and the poor, 3–8, 62

pragmatism: and feminist vocabulary, 81–82; William James and, 84

predestination, 6

progress, 91

prostitutes, 9

Proust, Marcel: on judging others, 2; *Sodome et Gomorrhe*, 76; *Le Temps retrouvé*, 1

Prussia: social estates in, 28

race: as baneful concept, 28; classification and definition of, 40, 41–45, 53–54; and "color," 75–76; and conflict, 52

Radical Philosophy (journal), 81

rationalism: and gender, 79; and humanism, 83

religion: and humanism, 83–84, 89

religious fundamentalism, 34, 50

revolution, 68

rights (human), 107

Robertson, J. M.: *The Saxon and the Celt*, 44

Rolland, Romain: *L'Annonciatrice*, 85–86

Rorty, Richard: *Contingency, Irony and Solidarity*, 32–34; "Feminism and Pragmatism," 80–82

Rousseau, Jean-Jacques, 91, 98–99

Russell, Bertrand, 1; *Principles of Social Reconstruction*, 27

Sade, Donatien Alphonse, marquis de, 103

Said, Edward: *Culture and Imperialism*, 68

Sartre, Jean-Paul: on existentialism as humanism, 86–89, 91; Foucault objects to, 106; Heidegger's critique of, 93–95; Lévi-Strauss rebuts, 95–100; *Critique de la raison dialectique*, 94; *L'Etre et le néant*, 30; *Existentialism Is a Humanism*, 91, 96; *La Nausée*, 30–31, 85–86; "Portrait of an Anti-Semite," 40

Saussure, Ferdinand de, 103, 113

Schiller, Ferdinand Canning Scott: *Humanism*, 84

Schopenhauer, Arthur, 29, 39–40

self: and difference, 113–14; Foucault on, 106; sense of, 68–69

Sellers, Wilfrid, 32

Serbs, 52–53

sex (gender): and differentiation, 73–82

Shaftesbury, Anthony Ashley Cooper, 7th Earl of, 58

Shakespeare, William: *King Lear*, 112–13

Shelley, Percy Bysshe, 46, 92
Sheridan, Alan: *Michel Foucault*, 68
Sinfield, Alan, 69–70
slaves, 34–35
Slavs, 43, 45, 53
Smith, Adam, 35
Socialism, 79
socialist humanism, 85–86
societies: as good, 23; origins of, 20–21. *See also* culture
Socrates, 26, 35
solidarity (human), 1, 31–33, 36
Solon, 108
Sophocles: *Antigone*, 15; *Philoctetes*, 15
Sorel, Georges, 92
Stalinism, 64, 86
state, the: impersonal nature of, 25–27; relation of individual to, 27; and revolution, 68. *See also* nation
Stefano, Christine di. *See* di Stefano, Christine
Steiner, George, 2
Strauss, Leo, 16
subcultures, 70
Swedenborg, Emanuel, 25

Tacitus, 45
Tel Quel (journal), 65
Tennyson, Alfred, 1st Baron, 41
Themistocles, 15
Thierry, Amédée: *Histoire des Gaulois*, 44
Third World, 47–48
Tolstoy, Count Leo: *What Then Must We Do?* 7–9
Tournier, Michel, 87
Toussaint L'Ouverture, Pierre-Dominique, 62–63

Toynbee Hall, London, 61–62
Trevor, J. C., 42–43
Trilling, Lionel, 60, 109
Turkle, Sherry, 65
Twain, Mark. *See* Finn, Huckleberry

United States of America: and European Community, 52
utilitarianism, 38
utopias, 21, 67, 102–3

values (moral). *See* moral values
Velasquez, Diego: *Las Meninas* (painting), 104
Vico, Giovanni Battista, 38
virtues, 14–15

Webb, Beatrice, 59, 61
Webb, Sidney, 58
"we-consciousness," 31–34
Wells, H. G., 91
Whitman, Walt: "Song of Myself," 39
William of Ockham, 51
Williams, Bernard: *Moral Luck*, 13
Wittgenstein, Ludwig, 6–7, 9, 109
women: Aristotle on, 35; work revalorized, 80–81. *See also* feminism
Wordsworth, Dorothy, 63
Wordsworth, William: on pleasure and benevolence, 63; *The Excursion*, 63; "Old Cumberland Beggar," 3–5, 62; "To Toussaint L'Ouverture," 62–63
world-state, 51–52

"Young England" movement, 57
Yugoslavia, 52–53